T0380192

Righteous Soul "Front Line"

righteous soul do real love,
wicked soul to creates righteous soul

SEONG JU CHOI

AuthorHouse™
1663 Liberty Drive
Bloomington, IN 47403
www.authorhouse.com
Phone: 1 (800) 839-8640

Because of the dynamic nature of the Internet, any web addresses or links contained in this book may have changed since publication and may no longer be valid. The views expressed in this work are solely those of the author and do not necessarily reflect the views of the publisher, and the publisher hereby disclaims any responsibility for them.

Any people depicted in stock imagery provided by Getty Images are models, and such images are being used for illustrative purposes only. Certain stock imagery © Getty Images.

This book is printed on acid-free paper.

ISBN: 978-1-7283-2878-2 (sc)
ISBN: 978-1-7283-2879-9 (e)

Print information available on the last page.

Published by AuthorHouse 09/26/2019

authorHOUSE®

Helping to read this book

Righteous soul living "front line" is that righteous soul living with wicked soul, so that righteous soul does survive but also create wicked soul to righteous soul, so then righteous soul keep righteous soul living energy creature and keep energy supply.

Righteous soul IN me living with wicked soul in the soul room, in the place righteous soul living in "front line",

Righteous soul living "front line" has variable livings.

Sometimes almost to disappeared hard and dangerous time and the other is somewhat bear of endure with wicked soul living "revenge and breaking righteous soul me", but all in the front line, must be survive and hear of broadcasting from righteous soul living in destination place, that is the creation of knowledge.

But truly wicked soul living is all from old knowledge, before living, so that if righteous soul do not supplied living in souls room then righteous soul living influenced of wicked soul old knowledge, here is old knowledge is old truth + mind getting much more than other, but also wicked soul "easy living" is mixed old knowledge effect to righteous souls, so that righteous soul living dangerous, so righteous soul keep hearing broadcasting from righteous soul living in destination place, of creation of knowledge supplied, so that this creation of knowledge effect in the soul room, then righteous soul living survive, and keep energy creating so that this righteous soul living energy to bear of endure with living wicked soul living.

Righteous soul living "front line" is only use creation of knowledge, then righteous soul do supplied to the wicked soul livings, wicked souls are all to be "easy living" then creation of knowledge is very swiftly adopt, so that righteous soul living is not effected strong of old truth with mind and wicked soul false knowledge not true so then righteous soul living is so hard, in the front line, righteous soul keep supplied to the front line, then righteous soul living survive.

This book "Righteous soul living "front line" is urgent living to me now also, because in the macro concept world also all based on old knowledge with contamination of mind living and wicked soul living of fall knowledge, so that righteous soul living s are not easy to live on, all wicked soul and mind living best place now in the macro concept world.

Truly this is so hard and dangerous to the micro concept world to macro concept world living

01234567890, of first 0 which is micro to macro then, righteous soul living is all front line, because righteous soul living survive, then the living knowledge all to be fitting wicked soul and mind living.

Righteous soul living by hearing broadcasting from righteous souls, so that get creation of knowledge to live righteous soul, this is all righteous soul front line.

This is how to wicked soul to be create

Wicked soul feel that strong wicked soul changed to infant of righteous soul, so that this change is all forgive from creator cosmos law, so that wicked soul to be righteous soul, then all of past orientated sinful, and wicked soul energy all to be used up, while in the front line of righteous soul, wicked soul all used up of wicked soul energy, but to living energy required then here is front line, helped by righteous soul, so that wicked soul living energy used righteous soul living energy, so that while righteous soul energy using automatically creation of knowledge also getting, so that wicked soul old knowledge gradually disappeared to the wicked soul, in the end righteous soul of creation of knowledge occupied in the wicked soul, so then wicked soul getting know that, how to complete macro concept world voyage complete.

The way is only this way, if in this front line if not to be changed into creating righteous soul then, keep incomplete macro concept world, this is really urgent chance to me to live in righteous soul, this is helping by creation of knowledge with real love, this is really urgent do real love to the righteous soul, because righteous soul do real love lover, so that righteous soul create lover of wicked soul, the really best of best living place righteous soul living in destination place carry righteous soul of wicked soul, but to go for the righteous soul living in destination place, only righteous soul, so that righteous soul all effort to create righteous soul, so then, here is also righteous soul is urgent, so righteous soul all of energy all of doing real love, and all of creation of knowledge, supply because how hard to the wicked soul, because wicked soul all adult soul of wicked soul to now infant of righteous soul, this is changed from changed wicked soul to righteous soul.

This is disappeared to wicked soul, but created to righteous soul, then, this process is so hard to the wicked soul also, it must be wicked soul so fear of out of wicked soul easy living, but wicked soul all do by lover of righteous soul, so that in the righteous soul front line, wicked soul to be righteous soul infant, so then here is righteous soul creating righteous soul to be real baby of creation of knowledge.

Then here is righteous soul front line of righteous soul really dong real love created a new righteous soul to be helped and keep with righteous soul helping righteous soul, here is macro concept world, righteous soul keep "righteous soul shares time with baby of righteous soul and help baby of righteous soul, but also doing real love baby of righteous soul.

Here is great creation of knowledge is comes to me

Macro concept world righteous soul living is do real love lover of wicked soul, this is then righteous soul do like righteous soul of infant, do love that, this is real love, as the righteous soul front line righteous soul create wicked soul to righteous soul, this is truly righteous soul macro concept world living.

Righteous soul in the macro concept world front line is

At now perfectly wicked soul to be righteous soul, but created righteous soul is so weak in energy so that keep righteous soul doing righteous soul living behavior in the macro concept world, then so that righteous soul helping beginning righteous soul of "the poor

& righteous soul" keep growing to "righteous soul & nothing", then in the end same with now like righteous soul me, at now righteous soul souls same at last a creation of righteous soul to be adult righteous soul, then righteous soul me and create righteous soul of lover to be living in the macro concept world living in excitement and both lover of righteous souls will safe comeback to the righteous soul living in destination place.

Righteous soul front line is

Ultimate creating wicked soul lover to righteous soul, then created righteous soul do real love to righteous soul, so that micro concept world righteous soul living in destination place to seek in the macro concept world, so that the dangerous voyage start, but as the righteous soul front line, so that meet wicked soul but the wicked soul created by the righteous soul, so that righteous soul creator in the front lie a wicked soul of lover so that creator of righteous soul creating of righteous soul relationship is huge strong this is eternity living in the righteous soul living in destination place.

Truly this is how to do, I did not know but today

Creation of knowledge make me learning it, this is righteous soul front line to the wicked soul, righteous soul create front line to the wicked soul, to make wicked soul feel warm and comfortable so that wicked soul feel easy living, then as the wicked soul feeling is easy living then, righteous soul also living in the soul room.

This is righteous soul create front line to the wicked soul

Then, wicked soul living easy living, so then righteous soul feed righteous living energy to the wicked soul so that, here is wicked soul to be changed into infant of righteous soul, so that righteous soul do "it shares time with other, help other, but also doing real love other"

So then, righteous soul energy all feed to the baby of wicked soul,

This is righteous soul living, feeding righteous soul energy to the wicked soul, but of righteous soul infant, this is truly righteous soul living mission in the soul room, for the purpose of righteous soul survive all of effort to do righteous soul behavior "it shares time with other, help other but also doing real love other".

Here is why righteous soul front line is creating is comes out.

Righteous soul do create front line to the wicked soul of "revenge and breaking", so that at first righteous soul crate do not use wicked soul "revenge and breaking" this is first because righteous soul first living in the soul room.

Contents

Before and after

Before was end of living

After is now living

But inter of before and after

This is micro concept point -1/limitless) ~+1/limtless)

But also before and after, then here is "and" is must be between

So then "and" has before components and after components so then

This "and" is still before 50 + after 50= 100 is real living.

So called

Here is comes up

Righteous soul living front lime

How to build

Before and after

This is "and" is comes "and" is suffering or loss or lose the game or bankrupt or sickness of hard time"

Then how to run over the "and" is must be "forgive and doing real love"

Then, in the hard time forgive and doing real love

Then hard time origin is must be comes of revenge and breaking of wicked soul

So then, as the righteous soul do "forgive and real love" then, here is righteous soul living energy is increased.

All of cosmos law judgement is correction

Past origin of before all to be "forgive and doing real love"

Because in me of before "wicked soul" and mind is surged time built

So that there is no righteous soul so in the place is wicked soul living in destination place.

How to out of before of wicked soul, truly before if origin of past old knowledge so then, the time and space was

Wicked soul living in destination place

But "and" of hard time must be war, sickness, and lost, losing gamer all of hard thing comes

Then here is "after" of new creation of knowledge, so called next now living is righteous soul living

So then, all must be "forgive and doing real love"

Then begins after only

Then cosmos law all know truth

So that forgive and doing real love is living in after of righteous soul living in destination place living.

Before/after

Whose actor living in the before

Whose living of actor is after living?

Then here is

Before and after

How hard "and", but to me losing mobile phone is truly righteous soul living in destination place

As righteous soul me "forgive and real love of getting my mobile phone" then correctly

Being comes after living of new and creation of knowledge governing righteous soul me

So that after that creation of knowledge based righteous meditation comes
Here is main concerning is how to keep end of my macro concept world living
Then this new creation of real living of meditation will keep eternity excitement completion.
Before/after

Before and after only key is "forgive and doing real love"
Forgive and doing real love is open for the "after"

Righteous soul front line

Righteous soul front line

Righteous soul living with wicked soul

Righteous soul must be survive with wicked soul

Wicked soul must be trying to living in "easy living using revenge and breaking energy"

Here is Righteous soul is living in front line master

Truly here is wicked soul "revenge and breaking energy and righteous soul "doing real love" energy must be same so that here is "revenge and breaking of wicked soul energy 50: doing real love of righteous soul energy is50 so that both combined energy is 100

This is book "Righteous soul living "front line""

But here righteous soul master of living then, it must be living in the front line

Righteous soul must be living all of effort so that righteous soul can be hearing broadcasting because in the front line is righteous soul to be disappeared from wicked soul "revenge and breaking energy".

But righteous soul living all to be living in the front line

So then righteous soul will use "doing real love wicked soul"

But also wicked soul will use "revenge break righteous soul'

This is front line

So long of this book master of righteous soul how to live is survive and doing keep living.

Here is front line is

Master "righteous soul" moving and change all of living time existing

Because righteous front line is must be keep connect with cosmos law macro and micro effect orbit, so that righteous soul living must be survive micro and macro, so that Righteous soul living is keep in front line.

Here is front line is righteous soul 50 plus wicked soul 50 to be created righteous soul front line 100. Truly there is no living between righteous soul and wicked soul, here is sure of in the side of righteous soul front line face to the wicked soul.

Then front line of righteous soul must be watch by "creator in the righteous soul living in destination place"

Keep signal to righteous soul so then righteous soul can hear of broadcasting from righteous soul living in destination place. That is "creation of knowledge" this creation of knowledge is only righteous soul use.

But in this front line of righteous soul, just against of wicked soul is here is there is not front line concept so that wicked soul living is only living in "easy living" so that if some disturb wicked soul easy living then, coincidence occur of "revenge and breaking energy".

So that wicked soul "revenge and breaking energy" is urgent to the righteous soul, truly to the righteous soul is urgent problems to survive or not, but righteous soul do not strong against to wicked soul "revenge and breaking" but righteous soul has creative knowledge to solve the problems, then still righteous soul living tools to live is "doing real love wicked soul", then righteous soul front line living tools are "creature of knowledge" and "doing real love wicked soul".

In the front line righteous soul to wicked soul

Righteous soul do live righteous soul living behavior "it shares time with wicked soul, help wicked soul, but also doing real love wicked soul" this is new and learning by a wicked soul, so then righteous soul front line is righteous soul living way and wicked soul to be "easy living of using revenge and breaking" is not same.

Righteous soul living front line is "doing real love wicked soul" but also helping "creation of knowledge" and Righteous soul mission is "meet lover of wicked soul and do real love wicked to create righteous soul" just like that, all of righteous soul front line is all hard, here is hard is all urgent righteous soul also to be disappeared from wicked soul strong anger of revenge and breaking.

Here is Righteous soul front line is basically righteous soul living in the front line then, righteous soul energy 50 other wicked soul living energy 50 equal to 100 energy living, here is true is righteous soul is master.

So then here is energy 100 is keep creating energy, just like do not used up, but keep creating energy, here is righteous soul front line, in the front line is righteous soul living required pure 100% righteous soul living required.

Here is Righteous soul living is so hard living, so that "the poor & righteous soul" to "righteous soul & nothing", just living of righteous soul do not consuming energy, so that the living is survive and living in eternity.

Righteous soul living front line is all living of macro concept world, because wicked soul living is not simple, wicked soul living is also strong energy, even righteous soul get creation of knowledge of new energy, but as the righteous soul creating energy also used after it by wicked soul.

Righteous soul living front line is righteous soul all living is face as same as wicked soul to righteous soul to be equal energy, this is wicked soul living must be fear because of wicked soul reluctance move and changed, just wicked soul keep in "easy living" is premium golden rule, so then Righteous soul keep righteous soul to be changed from wicked soul to righteous soul, this is righteous soul living silent and clean clear living.

Righteous soul front line is righteous soul living normal living way.

Righteous soul front line only meet wicked soul, then righteous soul with living wicked soul then, direct righteous soul can do help wicked soul to be "creation of knowledge and doing real love", this is all of righteous soul living.

Righteous soul living mission of creator has been same, righteous soul mission is find lover of wicked soul to create wicked soul to righteous soul, this is eternity mission of righteous soul, so that righteous soul living all living is pure 100% of righteous soul "it shares time with wicked soul and helping wicked soul to be learn so that creation of knowledge helping but also doing real love wicked soul" this is adversely survive righteous soul living, so that righteous soul to wicked soul of front line is strong and truth.

Righteous soul living front line is real living itself.

Righteous soul direction to wicked soul but wicked soul to righteous soul, but the direction purpose is

Wicked soul is to be living in "easy living" but Righteous soul is keep running to the righteous soul living in destination place,

There is no way to the righteous soul living in destination place; the way is righteous soul front line, righteous soul living keep living with wicked soul.

So that righteous soul to survive with "wicked soul", it is not like with wicked soul "revenge and breaking righteous soul" of righteous soul to be disappeared but righteous soul to wicked soul is " it shares time with wicked soul and help wicked soul but also doing real love wicked soul", then righteous soul help creation of knowledge, so that create righteous soul in the macro concept world, because wicked soul must be complete of macro concept world living, then righteous soul help to be creating new righteous soul, but wicked soul fear of it, because wicked soul living in "easy living" in the macro concept world, so called here is easy living is "rich and wicked soul" so long, in the macro concept world living "easy living" is hard to be changed into the poor and righteous soul living.

Because righteous soul living also "the poor & righteous soul" keep growing to "righteous soul and nothing", so that wicked soul of rich to be changed into the "the poor & righteous soul" this is so hard, but righteous soul living in destination place safe returning but created in the macro concept world is righteous soul living completion so that beginning in the righteous soul living in destination place living station at living eternity with lover.

Righteous soul living front line is

Wicked soul of revenge and breaking energy defense also, so that righteous soul living in destination place must be living in segregate from wicked soul in the micro concept world, truly micro concept world is righteous soul living in destination place is complete of soul living, but wicked soul living in destination place is not complete living, so that wicked souls are wait to voyage to macro concept world but righteous soul living in destination place all to be stationed eternity living in the righteous soul living in destination place.

But wicked soul living in destination place

All of wicked soul anger of it, because wicked souls are not complete living.

So that righteous soul front lime is all connected with wicked soul, so righteous soul living front line is

Keep front line in the macro concept world.

Before of wicked soul all to be forgiven

In the macro concept world living actors are all living before and after, but truly do not out of before.

If now is after then run over before after, so not in the after, but how to run at after, is "forgive", at now living in the macro concept world living all did forgive then, clear of now living possible, but if not "forgive before of wicked soul" then now living all connected with "before wicked soul living".

Righteous soul know that because righteous soul keep a cosmos law rule which is effect macro concept world and micro concept world both world governing rule, so that Righteous soul knows that Righteous soul living behavior is "it shares time with other, help other, but also doing real love other" this is include in "forgive", if righteous soul do not know "forgive and doing real love" then how to running to the righteous soul living in destination place.

Here is "before of wicked soul all to be forgiven" is I got a creation of knowledge hearing broadcasting from righteous soul living in destination place.

Righteous soul runs to the righteous soul living in destination place is all of righteous soul living time is defined so that a second also to be unit "breath and decision and acting of result judged=Righteous soul living energy cell", if living in righteous soul then Righteous soul living energy cell is righteous soul energy increased but also energy saved for righteous soul running to the righteous soul living in destination place.

So then before of wicked soul and after of righteous soul running to the righteous soul living in destination place, after is keep hearing broadcasting from righteous soul living in destination place, so that after world is using creation of knowledge.

But before of wicked soul is not move but go around depend on old knowledge but also wicked soul did all of using "revenge and breaking" so that all of before livings are still connecting to the before living "revenge and breaking" so that even living now but now is not after still now is before living.

Truly before living of wicked soul did "revenge and breaking" so that before all of livings are damaged some of livings are disappeared macro concept world, then how to forget before of wicked soul "revenge and breaking" but all of righteous soul much more than important is "righteous soul safe returning to the righteous soul living in destination place" this is mission of why micro concept world to macro concept world, so then as like mind form macro concept world, righteous soul keep running to the righteous soul living in destination place, so righteous soul keep "before to righteous soul moving is also unit" but righteous soul as the "keep righteous soul behavior is "it shares time with other, help other but also doing real love other" the fully "forgive before of wicked soul" then there is no obstacles then righteous soul voyage on the orbit of righteous soul living in destination place.

Here is why forgive "before of wicked soul" this answer is simple, righteous souls move and changed as the voyage orbit, all are rule cosmos law so that if cosmos law is this, then righteous soul to be living in then, but cosmos law is that is then righteous soul to be changed and move to then, this is righteous soul living way, but wicked soul and mind is all do not do cosmos law knowledge because cosmos law is not all time to be "easy living" what wicked soul try to live all of time same, without change and move, but cosmos law is up and down and turbulence all of hard time and good time is changed moving, the righteous souls moving is not simple and easy so that, this righteous soul living way can't follow by the wicked soul and mind.

Still explain that why Righteous soul must forgive "before of wicked soul" is for the purpose of righteous soul moving and change living, if righteous soul doing not move and change then, at that time there is no righteous soul but moment there is wicked soul and mind living.

Righteous soul all "forgive and doing real love" this is absolute living, righteous soul living is keep "it shares time with other, help other but also doing real love other" this is books 15 books can explain, Righteous soul living of micro concept world is recognition and macro concept world "easy living" of recognition is not same.

But truly macro concept world living "easy living" never micro concept world righteous soul but wicked soul living in destination place, so long, in the cosmos law is basis of righteous soul living standard, if living in righteous souls living.

If living in righteous soul living then, the living is keep cosmos law keeping, so that if living in wicked soul and mind living is not keep in cosmos law, so then, they cannot move and changed.

Righteous soul livings moving and change is out of before only, so that to be out of before, it must all before living world wicked soul behavior, then wicked soul do not disturb righteous soul me running to the righteous soul living voyage on the orbit.

But Righteous soul do not forgive then, it already there is no righteous soul, but all to be wicked soul living, truly forgive wicked soul then, the position is righteous soul, attitude of wicked soul living and righteous soul living is difference, righteous soul living is macro concept world is connecting with micro concept world good place of righteous soul living in destination place of excitement livings and the place is righteous soul creator also there so that righteous soul voyage of moving is much more than important but wicked soul even from micro concept world wicked soul living in destination place, but do not want to go the place, so that wicked soul do not know how to do, in the macro concept world, but "easy living" in the macro concept world, where to go for wicked soul, wicked soul must be saved by righteous soul.

Truly before world wicked soul do not know only "revenge and breaking", but what they did do not know to the righteous soul point of view, so then this is as the Righteous soul, so then beyond of before now after in righteous soul, but all to be now in after then, Righteous soul did forgive "Before of wicked soul" so long, if macro concept world livings also it don't have to expect "before of wicked soul" being "feel sorry" even wicked soul did, then what is difference, this not me, the only righteous soul me "forgive and do real love" is being now in after living, but also after living me is truly, I'm an righteous soul living.

After is running to the righteous soul living in destination place, it must be soon being before, then it also righteous soul do forgive and doing real love wicked soul, this is "before after" connection of a kind of front line, so that as the righteous soul living in after, but still before is front line, so that righteous soul only do "forgive and doing real love wicked soul in before".

Righteous soul do front line with wicked soul

Micro concept world creating Righteous soul me, then Righteous soul me start righteous soul living in destination place meet wicked soul it can be express

01234567890, here first (0) is start from creation of righteous soul voyage in the micro concept world, so that last (0) of start voyage in the macro concept world, then Righteous soul meet last (0) before, so called then 9 after Righteous soul meets wicked soul who argue I have been waiting for long time in this wicked soul living in destination place, so that I have to go to the macro concept world to "revenge and breaking" but also why only you go, righteous soul you one and wicked soul me is one, I automatically go with you in the macro concept world voyage.

01234567890, here is micro concept world final of after 9 righteous soul meet wicked soul, so then here is righteous soul to be hard living beginning. This is micro concept world meet wicked soul, so that this is righteous soul front line with wicked soul in the micro concept world before beginning macro concept world living beginning.

Macro concept world minor of micro concept world wicked soul and righteous soul, from micro concept world but major of mind and body living. Here is

012345678901234567890, center "(0) is macro concept world beginning, but final (0) is macro to micro.

Center (0) start macro concept world then

From micro concept world; wicked soul, righteous soul

From macro concept world; mind and body

So long all of living actor structure is

From micro concept world; wicked soul, righteous soul + from macro concept world; mind, body,

= wicked soul, righteous soul +mind +body; macro concept world livings

So then macro concept world righteous soul me is

"Righteous soul me" me structure is changed

So that infers to as righteous soul me,

As mind moment to 1/, then activation of righteous soul, so righteous soul know that macro and micro concept world, but mind do not know micro concept world, there for mind is not care to the righteous soul, but righteous soul me is so urgent, righteous soul must be running to the righteous soul living in destination place, but in me still strong wicked soul me also, so then wicked soul do not know why righteous soul runs to the righteous soul me, then in the micro concept world, wicked soul create new righteous soul, this is righteous soul me strong mission also, so that in me wicked soul must be changed into righteous soul, this is righteous soul living feeling front line, here righteous soul front line is wicked soul to be being righteous soul, so that righteous soul me freely runs to the righteous soul living in destination place.

How to be built righteous soul front line with wicked soul in ME

Righteous soul living has the "doing real love energy" but wicked soul is "revenge and breaking energy" this is front line, so that Righteous soul to run to righteous soul living in destination place going is must be on the problems of wicked soul "revenge and breaking energy", how to do, righteous soul living, in the macro concept world.

Righteous soul feel keep hearing how to do front line with wicked soul strong "revenge and breaking energy"

Righteous soul living in the front line is must be infer that at first doing hearing broadcasting from righteous soul living in destination place, so called "creation of knowledge", but also righteous soul has the tool to live on is "doing real love "but also righteous soul front line with wicked soul, then here is wicked soul "revenge and breaking energy 50" + Righteous soul energy 50" = absolute value 100.

Then here is absolute 100 is both can use wicked soul and righteous soul both in the righteous soul to wicked soul front line, here is strong energy condensed front line, here is must be wicked soul disappeared or righteous soul disappeared of front line.

Righteous soul front line helper are righteous soul broadcasting of "creation of knowledge", this is difference wicked soul "the old knowledge" so that if righteous soul living actor do choose "the poor and righteous soul" then survive but wicked soul of "easy living in the macro concept world" then it must be here is disappeared righteous souls.

"Righteous soul do front line with wicked soul"

Here is infer that righteous soul me is now living in the righteous soul then

It must be "righteous soul me" must be hear broadcasting from righteous soul living in destination place so that getting "creation of knowledge" this knowledge is how to create wicked soul righteous soul, so that righteous soul me in me wicked soul must be being changed into righteous soul, this is huge time consuming, but in the end if create wicked to righteous soul, then righteous soul to be safe returning to the righteous soul living in destination place.

Here is wicked soul excitement and good feeling is by righteous soul do real love wicked soul, this doing real love of wicked soul then wicked soul feel excitement, here is new excitement to the wicked soul, because originality wicked soul excitement is getting "easy living" the wicked soul feel is excitement, but wicked soul "it shared time with wicked soul, help wicked soul and doing real love wicked soul" so that wicked soul feel excitement by righteous soul living behavior to the wicked soul, so that wicked soul feel new excitement, this excitement is wicked soul excitement is "easy living only wicked soul" here righteous soul excitement is different from wicked it, there is righteous soul living excitement is go with other.

So then righteous soul living front line with wicked soul is

As the righteous soul living behavior "it shares time with other, help other, but also doing real love other"

This righteous soul living behavior doing each other, so that Righteous soul me do righteous soul other, then other do righteous soul living behavior then this is IN me righteous soul front line must be help wicked soul to be righteous soul combined each other, this is all righteous soul has "doing real love other".

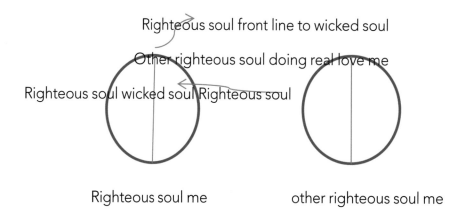

Righteous soul front line to wicked soul

Other righteous soul doing real love me

Righteous soul wicked soul Righteous soul

Righteous soul me   other righteous soul me

Righteous soul living behavior so that "righteous soul shares time with wicked soul, Righteous soul help wicked soul and righteous soul doing real love wicked soul"

So then

Righteous soul me righteous soul and wicked soul front line, other righteous soul doing righteous soul living behavior so that here is Righteous soul me, righteous soul living front line to be making wicked soul feeling excitement of good feeling.

But also Righteous soul me righteous soul hearing broadcasting from righteous soul of "creation of knowledge" then, it must be wicked soul me also, understand for easy living better old knowledge using "easy living" then wicked soul feel excitement better solving for easy living is "creation of knowledge" is better than old knowledge, so then "creation of knowledge" is also solved righteous soul living problems is "wicked soul to be righteous soul" so that righteous soul urgent to run to the righteous soul living in destination place.

Here is important creation of knowledge occurred

How to wicked soul to be creating is coincident with righteous soul doing possible running to the righteous soul living in destination place.

Here is righteous soul front line is absolute 100 is much more power wicked soul 50, or righteous soul 50, so that righteous soul me, to create wicked soul in ME, so that 100 energy input to create from wicked soul to righteous soul, so then this living in the macro concept world me living is must be

012345678901234567890, macro concept world living all the time use, going with meet macro concept world lover, so that righteous soul living front line with wicked soul of lover, so that righteous soul me do righteous soul living behavior to the wicked soul living lover, but also as same IN me solving ways to the macro concept world living because Righteous soul me being from "the poor & righteous" to "Righteous soul & nothing", now being "nothing" powerful doing real love wicked soul lover, so that already being "righteous soul & nothing"

Then Righteous soul me do real love strong to the wicked soul lover then, here is

Strong righteous soul "nothing" does real love both lover of wicked soul and lover of righteous soul, then

Lover of righteous soul to be strong righteous soul, but also lover of wicked soul feeling excitement so that keep changed into righteous soul, so here is strong righteous soul is powerful energy of righteous soul, so that string Righteous soul doing real love wicked soul and righteous soul, so then, getting strong righteous soul gain strong righteous soul so that wicked soul of lover, also lover of righteous soul front line forming, so then Righteous soul me righteous soul keep doing real love lover wicked soul, then much more than me being righteous soul being time is less than me.

Here is macro concept world living, if I living being of "righteous soul & nothing" then Righteous soul me help other being righteous soul is so easier.

Righteous soul front line to is very important to understand how to change IN me wicked soul righteous soul, and righteous soul mission lover create righteous soul.

Righteous soul front lines with "think of wicked soul"

Micro concept world righteous soul live with wicked soul in the micro concept world

Before beginning in macro concept world, macro concept world minor of soul form micro concept world is: righteous soul, wicked soul

But from macro concept world is mind and body

Righteous soul front line before think of wicked soul move to macro to saying and behavior of "revenge and breaking other"

So then now seen world macro concept world: saying, moving, action is all wicked soul of revenging and breaking

But truly righteous soul do hear of broadcasting from righteous soul living in destination place

So that creation of knowledge is from hearing broadcasting from righteous soul living in destination place

In the macro concept world all of livings are moving and saying and cry all variance and change all move

This is out of thinking of wicked soul; just "creation of knowledge" is righteous soul here broadcasting so then

This creation of knowledge is solving closing gate, so that this is righteous soul of "creation of knowledge"

Righteous soul runs to the righteous soul living in destination place.

So then

Hearing broadcasting from righteous soul living in destination place is

Only in the righteous soul livings hearing, so then in the macro concept world righteous soul me is kind of still runs to the righteous soul living in destination place

So that righteous soul living is follow creation of knowledge, this is cosmos law, so that this is natural law also so that

Righteous soul living actor is a knows of nature, so that this is in the macro concept world creation of world and righteous soul

is same, but moving of follow of think of wicked soul behavior of "revenge and breaking" is in the same of micro concept world

Righteous soul front line same.

So then righteous soul living actor of creation of knowledge run for the righteous soul living in destination place of

Eternity living because righteous soul living is creation of knowledge of truth, cosmos law keep so that righteous soul

From to the wicked soul is macro and micro same.

So called micro concept world also righteous soul is circumstance but also macro concept world also

Do not changed circumstance of me.

By the circumstance living, moving all to be wicked souls

Righteous soul me being circumstance of the wicked souls in cosmos law influenced macro concept world and micro concept world. This is a Righteous soul front line under the cosmos law influenced

Here is Righteous soul front line with wicked soul, a creation of knowledge.

Righteous soul and wicked soul front line is both macro and micro concept world both time and space are effect, so called that cosmos law is influence living place all to be effective.

Righteous soul livings in the macro concept world, then

When meet righteous soul living actor meet wicked soul living actor then, here is front line is created so between wicked soul and righteous soul, both feeling, so then, wicked soul understanding scripture is "revenge and breaking energy" but righteous soul scripture must be "doing real love wicked soul".

Then wicked soul try to live in "easy living" now in the front line with Righteous soul, so then, wicked soul feel hard then it must be using of "revenge and breaking energy" then here is righteous soul "doing real love" is not act so that, wicked soul do not feel in warm and feeling good, so that infer that Righteous soul to be front line with wicked soul, then, it must be wicked soul do not feel hard but peace, so then wicked soul do not use "revenge and breaking energy" so all goes to wicked soul keep in "easy living" while meeting Righteous soul.

How to do,

There is no wicked soul hard living meeting righteous soul, but truly wicked soul revenge righteous soul, because wicked soul do not know "creation of knowledge", wicked soul do not have rule to "it shares time with other, help other, and doing real love other", so that wicked soul meets righteous soul do on the way of wicked soul living old knowledge way, deceit, segregate, discriminate etc. so that wicked soul living and righteous soul living is difference so that, wicked soul feel strange with righteous soul livings.

How to do righteous soul in the front line with wicked soul

Then, it must be in the time of "the poor & righteous soul" then it must be living of poor living is not like by wicked soul so that, in the place poor living is survive from wicked soul "revenge and breaking" so that righteous soul living, to survive in the macro concept world is so hard poor living, then, the living is distance from wicked soul "revenge and breaking" but righteous soul to be living in "righteous soul & nothing" then, here is difference, because macro concept world wicked soul living meet "righteous soul & nothing" then, it is the macro concept world living all to be seen as the "mind+ body with wicked soul, or righteous soul" etc., so that all is same but to the seen by the micro concept world is seen as the wicked soul living actor and righteous soul living actor.

Here is macro concept world, wicked soul meet "righteous soul & nothing" then, here is language expression is "righteous soul & nothing" but true in the real meet "wicked soul to righteous soul" then it must be "wicked soul meet a nothing" here is very important thing is "righteous soul & nothing= nothing" this nothing is in the micro concept world is major living actor of righteous soul.

Here is macro concept world front line is created

Wicked soul meet "righteous soul & nothing= noting" then in the macro concept world wicked soul meet righteous soul, then, there is no burden and just feel in excitement with meeting righteous soul, because there is not target to be "revenge and breaking" so that, it don't necessary using wicked soul "revenge and breaking energy".

Because wicked soul meet righteous soul but, wicked soul feels that here is only wicked soul me only, so that wicked soul feels warm and good.

Truly here is righteous soul is not here, in the seen macro concept world, no, macro concept world, body is seen, but righteous soul body is must be harmony with circumstance, so that even righteous soul living actor in here but wicked soul living actor feel fragrance of perfume of flower from righteous soul living actor.

So then "righteous soul & nothing" living is understand as feel fragrance of perfume of flower, even there is still righteous soul me in the seen to the wicked soul living actor.

Here is what is feeling fragrance of perfume of flower of righteous soul & nothing?

Here is "righteous soul &nothing" behavior of creation of knowledge which hearing from righteous soul living in destination place, so that wicked soul feel in the front line with righteous soul & nothing is feeling of just time and space of wicked soul, so that here is righteous soul to be time and space of wicked soul, so righteous soul living is not moving but living in eternity same of truth of creation of knowledge living behavior.

Here is difference between wicked soul and righteous soul is wicked soul living in the old knowledge in the past, but righteous soul living is the truth of creation of knowledge in the micro concept point (-1/ ~+1/), so that wicked soul understanding in the front line with "righteous soul & nothing" is feeling in the time and space of righteous soul, so that righteous soul is do not change of eternity of being circumstance.

In this front line is really urgent but necessary righteous soul to wicked soul is based on creation of knowledge, righteous soul in the front line to be create wicked soul to righteous soul so that this is not simple, but keep make wicked soul to be feel in creation of knowledge understanding, so then, Righteous soul living actor must be living in solving all of old knowledge problems solving helper to the wicked soul, as the keep doing righteous soul living behavior of " it shares time with other on the creation of knowledge, help wicked soul based on the truth of creation of knowledge, in the end, very important is doing real love wicked soul as the strong righteous soul living energy of truth and creation of knowledge".

So then here is "righteous soul and nothing" must be thorough hearing broadcasting from righteous soul living in destination lace, so that here is truth is "righteous soul & nothing" is in the living of righteous soul living in destination place on the macro concept world, so that on the macro concept world, micro concept world righteous soul living in destination place is in the "righteous soul & nothing" righteous soul actor IN.

Creature of front line with wicked soul is creature of Energy

Micro concept world front line is always between wicked soul and Righteous soul. In this place is urgent to the righteous soul, because righteous soul living is keep moving and keep change so then, righteous soul living energy need to move to righteous soul living in destination place.

This energy all of created between in the front line between wicked soul and righteous soul, so then how to righteous soul righteous soul living energy, this is righteous soul living behavior; "it shares time with other, and help other but also doing real love other",

Here is Righteous soul meet wicked soul, so then here is created righteous soul front line with wicked soul, so then wicked soul meet also front line, so then wicked soul is in the front line all try to get at "easy living" positon so that wicked soul also use based on old knowledge and wicked soul energy, so that both energy all meet in the front line.

Front line between righteous soul and wicked soul

Righteous soul 50	Wicked soul 50
Creature of knowledge	Old knowledge
Doing real love other	Revenge and breaking other
It shares time with other, help other, doing real love	Only "easy living"

Front line

Front line = Righteous soul 50 + wicked soul 50 = 100

In the front line energy is 100

Here is conflict between creatures of knowledge to old knowledge

Doing real love to Revenge and breaking

And it shares time with other; help other and real love other to only "easy living"

Righteous soul front line is to be circumstance of wicked soul

So then even here front line is exist but there is no to the wicked soul, \

There is no creative soul, doing real love, but also it shares time with other, help other, it shares time with other, so that wicked soul to be living of

Old knowledge revenge and breaking other, but also doing "easy living"

But here front line is meeting in the place of righteous soul master and host front line then

Righteous soul do not appeared to the wicked soul, but truly only to the wicked soul, but cosmos law see righteous soul, but here is very important because righteous soul to be in this place, keep hearing broadcasting from righteous soul living in destination place

So that now in the front line is suppled to righteous soul, creation of knowledge, this knowledge is same as the cosmos law so then, here is righteous soul is truly truth of knowledge so that, this living is do not changed but to be being to the circumstance, so that wicked soul move freely but also, used wicked soul has, here is wicked soul will learn righteous soul livings.

This is righteous soul feel in excitement

Here is front line is

Righteous soul creation of knowledge wicked soul old knowledge

Righteous soul doing real love wicked soul Revenge and breaking other

Righteous soul behavior of "it shares time with other, help other but also doing real love other"

Wicked soul "only easy living"

Here front line of righteous soul meet wicked soul, then righteous soul of master and host is at first doing righteous soul living behavior "it shares time with wicked soul, help wicked soul and doing real love wicked soul", so then this is only righteous soul to do wicked soul in the front line with wicked soul of "revenge and breaking" this is urgent to the righteous soul, but righteous soul, there is no mind, there is no me, so that righteous soul to be with front line with wicked soul is survive and dong real love wicked soul just in the circumstance for the wicked soul, here is front line of righteous soul.

Righteous soul front line is not a short time but longtime with front lien with wicked soul so then

Righteous soul living of moving and runs and changed voyage in the orbit to the righteous soul living in destination place, then here is need righteous soul survival energy even running to the righteous soul living in destination place, so that energy getting is here of Righteous soul host of front line with wicked soul, here is righteous soul righteous soul living behavior is same as cosmos law, so that here in the front line righteous soul keep share with wicked soul, and help wicked soul and doing real love wicked soul, here all to be "breath and decision action of righteous soul after then judged as righteous soul living energy"

Here is Righteous soul living energy is in the front line with wicked soul, so that righteous soul living keep hearing creation of knowledge to meet every case of wicked soul meeting do righteous soul living behavior and creation of knowledge to the wicked soul of old knowledge.

Wicked soul old knowledge changed by before of righteous soul's creation of knowledge so that wicked soul can use creation of knowledge help to wicked soul so that wicked soul use creation of knowledge, then this is only possible in the righteous soul master of front line with wicked soul.

Here is master of righteous soul front line with wicked soul, then wicked soul can be used same as righteous soul hearing broadcasting from righteous soul living in destination place, of creation knowledge so then, wicked soul old knowledge must be solved as adopt righteous soul of creation of knowledge.

Here is righteous soul to be feel excitement with wicked soul to be used righteous soul of creation of knowledge, so then, wicked soul can be feel, micro concept world righteous soul living in destination place living indirectly.

This is very important to the righteous soul of mission carried

Righteous soul mission is "find lover and the lover of wicked soul to be created as righteous soul so that righteous soul with lover of created righteous soul of lover to be living in the righteous soul living in destination place"

Macro concept world is wicked soul to be created to the righteous soul, to the righteous soul meet a wicked soul of lover, then righteous soul do front line with wicked soul; this front line is righteous soul master of host front line with lover of wicked soul.

Here is righteous soul to wicked soul lover front line is built by righteous soul

So then righteous soul master and host of front line is "meet wicked soul who is to be love and living in the righteous soul living in destination place", origin of righteous soul know that how living is excitement in the righteous soul living n destination place, so that righteous soul is urgent to create lover of wicked soul.

Righteous soul to wicked soul of lover front line is urgent living

So then, infer that who is the righteous soul between now living me in macro concept world, so then whether me other lover is do not know, to be living in righteous soul living them, it must be sure is righteous soul living me is important as the me, to be living as the righteous soul living, it is sure of possible saving a lover of wicked soul, then this is both living complete;

Truly wicked soul of wicked soul must be saved from me, as the my righteous soul front line with wicked soul of lover, sure of it, lover also has the wicked soul energy, if not me in righteous soul, then it is not sure of lover is in the wicked soul or not, so that it must important is being righteous soul living is urgent.

Righteous soul front line with creator in the righteous soul living in destination place

Righteous soul created by creator in the righteous soul living in destination place. So then righteous soul and creator front line was built, here is creator is master front line with created righteous soul.

Creating righteous soul in the righteous soul living in destination palace is feeling in silent clean clear.

Creator try to do help righteous soul, so that creator help living tools after leaving only depend on is "doing real love other of wicked soul" this is only righteous soul living way.

So then righteous soul and creator front line is creator feeling excitement with righteous soul but try to do creator with to do righteous soul living behavior "creator time with creator and help righteous soul but also creator do real love righteous soul", so then here is righteous soul and creator energy both together righteous soul energy is 100.

Creator energy also righteous soul living energy 50

Both combined to = creator righteous soul energy 100= righteous soul righteous soul energy 100

Righteous soul also righteous soul living energy 50

Here is righteous soul living in destination living in destination place, both creator and righteous soul is all to be in the righteous soul living in destination place, creator know both macro and micro so creator completer micro and macro living, infer that safe returning to righteous soul living in destination place, so then, being creator role of creating righteous soul.

Then here is creator is truth of creation of knowledge creating role, so that if creating righteous soul to be also safe returning to the righteous soul living in destination place, creator also do righteous soul behavior "creator time with voyage righteous soul and help righteous soul to solve the problems, but also doing creator do real love righteous soul keep in righteous soul, in the hard time with wicked soul" this is creator to righteous soul is combined to energy 100.

Righteous soul front line with creator is all depend on creator, but also righteous soul feel in excitement with creator help righteous soul, creator to be voyaged micro to macro is also excitement.

So then creator and righteous soul if righteous soul voyaged in the cosmos law of orbit then creator and creator go with, then endless give broadcasting how to solve now problems, so that righteous soul hear and getting creation of knowledge, but also keep real loving righteous soul by creator, then this is real excitement, but also in the hard time with wicked soul in the soul room, but still creator doing real love righteous soul, so then, righteous soul feel excitement then, keep runs from macro to micro of righteous soul living in destination place.

Infer that

At now living me is so hard then

Try to live righteous soul living me, then, as can hear broadcasting from righteous soul living in destination place, but also get a creation of knowledge with doing real love form creator.

Truly now living in macro concept world me is

Helped hearing broadcasting so that I can hear of broadcasting so now book writing, to me is book writing is problems so then, I can hear of broadcasting then hear of result is "creation of knowledge" so I am just hear and writing only, all is from creator of righteous soul me.

Creator keep broadcasting solving problems and running to the righteous soul livening in destination place.

"Righteous soul front line with creator in the righteous soul living in destination place"

Infer that righteous soul front line with creator then

Creator keep with righteous soul "creator shares time with righteous soul, and creator help righteous soul but also creator do real love righteous soul" this is all going with voyage of righteous soul.

This is righteous soul font line strong

So that righteous soul front line with wicked soul, then now living of righteous soul front line with creature so that righteous soul front line with wicked soul also endure with it.

Creator and righteous soul front line is righteous soul energy is 100 so that, creator role is with righteous soul then, itself is righteous soul living energy in the voyage is 100, so that righteous soul front line with creature then, creature must be being of righteous soul circumstance, righteous soul with creator then, righteous soul feel in excitement with creator.

Truly righteous soul with creator gain energy and keep in righteous soul living energy, so then in the voyage hard with but also needed creator energy then, righteous soul front line with creature, at this time, creator front line is all effort to do " creator shares time with righteous soul, help righteous soul, but also doing real love righteous soul"

Then righteous soul will complete from micro to macro and final safe comeback to the righteous soul living in destination place.

Righteous soul front line with wicked soul, between micro concept world and macro concept world

As living in righteous soul then there is wicked soul, so then here is comes up righteous soul and wicked soul front line.

if safe living in the only righteous soul to righteous soul the, the place front line is both righteous soul to righteous soul, here also has if righteous soul then here is also minor of wicked soul existed to that here is front line is also created.

but also in the living as wicked soul then, in the major of wicked soul front line with other front line but here is also has the minor of righteous soul is, this is front line must be produced.

but here is "righteous soul front line with wicked soul" then in this front line must be so hard with living righteous soul to wicked soul, but here is both strong energy wicked soul 50, and righteous soul energy 50 is front line so then here is front line energy is 100.

In this front line is in the micro concept world

So then, wicked soul has from wicked soul living in destination place, living tool "revenge and breaking energy", Righteous soul has from righteous soul living in destination place "doing real love energy".

so that in this micro concept world living in the macro concept world, so called macro concept world body, so then micro concept world cosmos, so long here is macro concept world soul room.

Here is created of righteous soul to wicked soul front line.

So then, here is front line is

Wicked soul "revenge and breaking energy" 50 + righteous soul "doing real love energy" 50=100 is in the front line is created at the macro concept world, but truly here is Seen world unseen wicked soul and righteous soul is in front line living.

So then, there is

wicked soul «revenge and breaking energy» 50 to be seen in the macro concept world of doing "easy living", so then try to be living in only wicked soul try to live in easy living.

righteous soul "doing real love energy" 50 to be seen in the macro concept world of "the poor & righteous soul living", so then righteous soul living behavior is "it shares time with other, help other but also doing real love other".

So long here is righteous soul front line to wicked soul then,

"Doing real love wicked soul of revenge and breaking energy"

Wicked soul front line with righteous soul then

"Doing revenge and breaking to righteous soul"

Because wicked soul only know "revenge and breaking" with old knowledge

Righteous soul "know doing real love with creation of knowledge

So then

In the front line is

"Revenge and breaking with old knowledge" 50 energy + "doing real love with creation of knowledge" 50 = 100.

In the front line doing, then

Wicked soul know creation of knowledge and righteous soul know old knowledge

So then, there is

In the forint line creates new energy and new knowledge.

So long all of front line is move and changed so that, this is micro concept world living, then

Macro concept world living actor character is so huge numbers of difference livings are created in the macro concept world.

Here is macro concept world front line is energy 100 is youth time, must be, so then here is

Front line is string power of energy is combined end create variable knowledge

Wicked soul old knowledge combined to righteous soul creation of knowledge

So this time front line energy is must be 100 all to the youth.

As the time is passed then

Infer of it, in the micro concept world

Righteous soul do strong do real love wicked soul, then wicked soul learn of righteous soul creation of knowledge then, but also righteous soul doing real love, so then, a wicked soul accept righteous soul real love and creation of knowledge then, here is wicked soul follow to the righteous soul livings so then, in the soul room, created wicked soul to be righteous soul, so then here is original righteous soul and created righteous soul meet then, here is strong righteous soul living appeared up,

In this time macro concept world me is righteous soul me, so then, again the righteous soul energy is only righteous soul 50 + create righteous soul 50= strong righteous soul, then here is

Appeared up of "righteous soul & nothing"

Here is Righteous soul me, so then macro concept world me is righteous soul me, but also" righteous soul & nothing".

But in this time there is no wicked soul, so that out of front line with wicked soul, but in this time

Righteous soul front line with wicked soul is "righteous soul & nothing" to other wicked soul in the macro concept world, so long, macro concept world other wicked soul front line comes.

So long, in the macro concept world righteous soul being perfect righteous soul me, then

There is created with macro concept world other of wicked soul, so then, here is

"righteous soul & nothing" + other wicked soul in the macro concept world" = so that

Here is strong righteous soul of righteous soul me do real love wicked soul macro concept world so then, righteous soul & nothing keep strong "creation of knowledge" to the wicked soul of macro concept world other.

As Righteous soul & nothing = righteous soul me

Then this living is me, so then me create front line with macro concept world of love of wicked soul so then,

Macro concept world create front line

Righteous soul me to wicked soul lover then here automatically lover of wicked soul to be created as the righteous soul, so long, here is Righteous soul me and create loved of righteous soul

Living in the righteous soul living.

But here is must know that

Macro concept world righteous soul me energy 50 + lover of wicked soul energy 50 = 100

this living is in the macro concept world living, time, but here is righteous soul me doing string real love and creature of knowledge to wicked soul of lover then, wicked soul lover to be being created as the righteous soul living.

So then here is righteous soul of originality righteous soul me, know that what is do in the macro concept world that is mission clear, mission has been doing "macro concept world righteous soul lover creating then, safe returning with lover to the righteous soul living in destination place"

But the righteous soul "me" and lover of righteous soul to be living in the righteous soul living in destination place in eternity living, living in the righteous soul living in destination place eternity.

Front line from micro to macro

Front line of micro concept world

Before comes to the macro concept world meet in the macro concept world soul room, this is micro concept world front line in the point of view righteous soul front line to the wicked soul. So then in the front line if righteous soul do real love wicked soul, then micro concept world soul to be appeared to righteous soul, but if wicked soul do "revenge and breaking to righteous soul" so that wicked soul only appeared then wicked soul appeared up.

Here is Righteous soul appeared up then, original righteous soul living in the macro concept world, but wicked soul appeared up then original righteous soul to be disappeared, so that macro concept world righteous soul and micro concept world righteous soul creator line also disappeared.

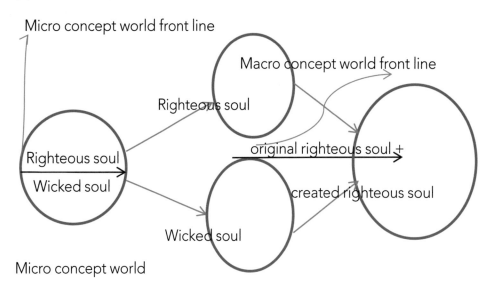

Micro concept world front line

Macro concept world front line

Righteous soul

Righteous soul
Wicked soul

original righteous soul +

created righteous soul

Wicked soul

Micro concept world

Macro concept world

Micro concept world Righteous soul
Living in destination place

Micro concept world front line in the soul room, here is condition

In the point of righteous soul front line to wicked soul, then here is righteous soul appeared

But in the point of wicked soul front line to righteous soul, then here is wicked soul appeared

If survived righteous soul in the soul room then, in the macro concept world living actor in original righteous soul in the macro concept world living, but if survive as the wicked soul living, the living in the macro concept world is wicked soul living actor.

So long, in the macro concept world Righteous soul of original from micro concept world righteous soul living in destination place, so long original righteous soul know that because righteous soul can hear broadcasting from righteous soul living in destination place, so long here is righteous soul mission is "meet a wicked soul of lover meet and do real love wicked soul then create righteous soul" this is why righteous soul voyage to the macro concept so hard working.

So that here is

Macro concept world meet wicked soul living actor

In the macro concept world righteous soul front line with wicked soul so that righteous soul do real love wicked soul living actor with helping creation of knowledge to solve lover of wicked soul face problems.

Macro concept world front line is

Righteous soul living me and wicked soul living actor of lover front line is created in the macro concept world.

Then original righteous soul keep doing real love and help learning creation of knowledge to wicked soul lover so that wicked soul of love to be created new righteous soul in the macro concept world, so then, here is righteous soul and wicked soul of lover front line, in this front line created righteous soul living of lover.

So then, in the macro concept world, to be saved from righteous soul of lover, so that wicked soul must to be living with righteous soul living actor. This is macro concept world real important living, because as the mission of righteous soul so that as the righteous soul to wicked soul to be saved infer that one to one, so if righteous soul surviving in the macro concept world soul room, then a new righteous soul will be created in the macro concept world righteous soul front line with wicked soul living actor then, righteous soul do real love wicked soul and help creation of knowledge the lover of wicked soul.

In the end wicked soul of lover to be in the righteous soul living actor, this is real important why here is macro concept world front line, here is all of front line is not easy, the righteous soul do real love wicked soul so hard but righteous soul all do real love wicked soul, this is righteous soul living in the macro concept world.

Front line is micro and macro concept world all to be created, so that in the front line all to be created, here is macro concept world, must live with creating front line, then here is macro concept world living mission carry out.

Righteous soul and wicked soul front line is necessary in the macro concept world.

Wicked soul old knowledge front line to righteous soul creation of knowledge

Wicked soul old knowledge based on "think of wicked soul", so then this is also "think of wicked soul past origin revenge and breaking accident and one thing keep supplied" so then wicked soul all depend on old knowledge.

But righteous soul keep running to the righteous soul living in destination place, so then here is from micro concept world of righteous soul to macro concept world voyage to meet lover of wicked soul to create lover to be righteous soul of mission clear then righteous soul lover bring to the righteous soul living in destination place of micro concept world.

So then to the righteous soul living problems is running to the future not past, so that righteous soul here is future then, now living is not in future so that in the micro concept point (-1/~+1/), meet future problems solving of creation of knowledge, then this is in the feeling of macro concept world living me, feel hearing broadcasting from righteous soul living in destination place, this is difference from "think of wicked soul" which remind wicked soul me to do "revenge and breaking others" but righteous soul hearing broadcasting all for righteous soul living runs to the righteous soul living in destination problems solving .

"Wicked soul old knowledge front line to righteous soul creation of knowledge"

Wicked soul old knowledge front line to righteous soul creation of knowledge is very important because righteous soul doing real love wicked soul with helping wicked soul of righteous soul problems solving of creation of knowledge.

Because righteous soul save wicked soul who do not know runs to the righteous soul living in destination place going knowledge do not know, so that righteous soul do real love wicked soul with creation of knowledge.

Truly righteous soul hearing broadcasting from righteous soul living in destination place so that, the creation of knowledge is true and real and just living it, but to the wicked soul of creation of knowledge is do not know, all because wicked soul all depend on old knowledge, so that all try to believe that old knowledge, so that wicked soul livings are all good at memorizing so that wicked souls are "easy living possible" because do not memorize then, problems solving is impossible, but also higher ranking problems solving is impossible, so then wicked soul old knowledge is power to the wicked soul so that wicked soul do not believe that creation of knowledge.

But righteous soul do not believe that solving now running to the righteous soul living in destination problems do not solve the problems, so that creation of knowledge which is hearing broadcasting from righteous soul living in destination place.

So then here is wicked soul old knowledge to righteous soul creation of knowledge front line is clear.

Old knowledge to creation of knowledge front line, so that living on the old knowledge with structure of livings and there is no structure but righteous soul of creation of knowledge, then in the macro concept world, macro concept world mind and wicked soul using old knowledge is mightier than righteous soul creation of knowledge.

This means that wicked soul old knowledge do not know righteous soul creation of knowledge, so that here is wicked soul do not know creation of knowledge so that "the poor & righteous soul" safe growing in the corner of the macro concept world, so that "the poor & righteous soul can hear broadcasting from righteous soul living in destination place" but wicked soul only rely on "thinking of wicked soul of old knowledge" so that, in the macro concept world all mixed living wicked soul, righteous soul, mind and body nut all to be living possible, because living knowledge is not same wicked soul is based on past of old knowledge but righteous soul is future of creation of knowledge.

But here is righteous soul based on creation of knowledge must be create front line with wicked soul old knowledge based on living.

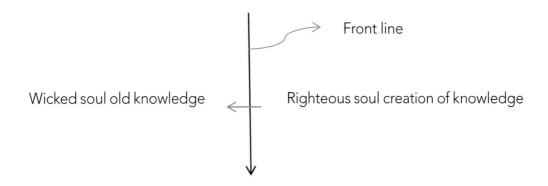

Righteous soul creation of knowledge front line to wicked soul old knowledge

Wicked soul old knowledge to righteous soul creation of knowledge front line is wicked soul do not get creation of knowledge because it don't necessary and do not know creation of knowledge but also do not there is creation of knowledge so that wicked soul truly hard to know righteous soul creation of knowledge so that, in the macro concept world living mind and wicked souls are all living based on old knowledge.

But truly in the micro concept world seen now macro concept world living

Then even wicked soul, and mind do living on the old knowledge but, truly all their livings are all depend on mixed with old knowledge and creation of knowledge.

In the front line must be

Old knowledge + creation of knowledge = now living in the macro concept world living actor.

But here is who living on the creation of knowledge or who is living based on old knowledge is righteous soul living or wicked soul and mind living.

But here is important is

In the front line appeared up of creation of righteous knowledge, so that wicked soul also get a knowledge with righteous soul doing real love wicked soul, this is real important truth.

As the doing real love is

Righteous soul do real love wicked soul then wicked soul feel in excitement, this is doing real love, so that macro and micro righteous soul do real love in me out me both so then, while doing real love wicked soul then, carry the creation of knowledge.

Righteous soul "doing real love" is "creation of knowledge"

Wicked soul "doing revenge and breaking" is "old knowledge"

So that in the front line

Righteous soul "doing real love" is "creation of knowledge" + Wicked soul "doing revenge and breaking" is "old knowledge" = wicked soul feeling is excitement and getting know creation of knowledge.

Here is important is "creation of knowledge" front line with "old knowledge" is benefit is wicked soul, because in the feeling of macro concept world then, wicked soul feeling excitement is excitement.

Truly righteous soul is helping wicked soul to use creation of knowledge then, why wicked soul feel in excitement is solve the hard problems, so that wicked soul past unsolved problems solved, this is wicked soul get a known, righteous soul "real love with creation of knowledge" is really wicked soul living getting better.

So then wicked soul getting use righteous soul of creation of knowledge

This is means that righteous soul of creation of knowledge is effective in the front line, so long, front line is necessary with righteous soul do solve mission clear but also wicked soul create of righteous soul, so this macro concept world living front lines are all to be required.

"Wicked soul old knowledge front line to righteous soul creation of knowledge" in the end wicked soul know righteous soul creation of knowledge, this is solved wicked soul from past of old knowledge do not solve problems, this hard problems solved by a righteous soul of creation of knowledge.

Then here is wicked soul past old knowledge must be solved only by creation of knowledge of righteous soul, so then, how to live in the macro concept world is decide.

If to be righteous souls runs righteous soul living in destination place, righteous soul front line with wicked soul is necessary and required.

Righteous soul wicked soul must keep in front line, then in the front line all of problems to be solved from past old knowledge unsolved problems.

Righteous soul front line to the wicked soul wicked soul to be feel in excitement but also gradually being in righteous soul, just only to do righteous soul for the wicked soul

Front line is wicked soul to righteous soul, righteous soul to wicked soul, here is balance is no one damaged but in the balance keeps running in the front line. But here is front line is very required to do righteous soul and wicked soul meet then here is must be if someone to be the other circumstance then all to be survive do use their energy then, truly righteous soul to be disappeared because wicked soul "revenge and breaking energy" truly righteous soul to be disappeared.

So then in this front line, righteous soul must be being wicked soul living circumstance

So then, wicked soul still strong energy, but righteous soul only has doing real love only, so then here is doing real love is, "doing real love" is do real love create a new excitement wicked soul and righteous soul, but also doing real love is long time routine "forgive and forgive and doing real love" so then, here is righteous soul to be living in the circumstance is doing now move, but do live "it shares time wicked soul, help wicked soul, but also doing real love wicked soul", so then this is must be long time but also long time to be circumstance to the wicked soul, so then wicked soul living still front line with righteous soul.

Righteous soul Front line to wicked soul

Righteous soul is tool only, because wicked soul know clearly when righteous soul do real love wicked soul then, the wicked soul to be living do not use wicked soul energy of "revenge and breaking", doing real love is "forgive and doing real love but also help righteous soul of creating knowledge" so that as keep time used but long time righteous soul do real love with helping creature of knowledge.

As the righteous soul keep front line with wicked soul

Wicked soul also to be front line is "revenge and breaking of old knowledge energy" keep accept righteous soul of creation of knowledge, but also while, wicked soul "revenge and breaking of past origin" become dilute, because

If wicked soul do "revenge and breaking" all of macro concept world living, then again do not complete righteous soul living, so getting know that by accept front line with righteous soul, righteous soul doing real love wicked soul with creation of knowledge "righteous souls now running for the righteous soul living in destination place, so that wicked soul front line to the righteous soul then, wicked soul know that how to complete living in the macro concept world as being righteous soul living, who is just living in righteous soul then automatically safe returning to the righteous soul living in destination place.

But wicked soul now only depend on old knowledge, so that wicked soul living based on "easy living", here is righteous soul "creation of knowledge" is not help to live in "easy living" but righteous soul creation of knowledge is still runs to the righteous soul living in destination place going problems solving.

Wicked soul based on old knowledge "easy living", righteous soul "creation of knowledge of running to the righteous soul living in destination place, this is also front line, so then righteous soul must be there is no remaining "easy living", but all running for the righteous soul living in destination place, so that, righteous soul living is not heavy but light, so that righteous soul living is "it shares time with other, help other, but also doing real love other", all of energy must be used this routine, then righteous soul to b living in light for running best.

Wicked soul old knowledge depend on "easy living" is keep weight so then, this is there is no necessary because wicked soul do not know, in the micro concept world not wicked soul livening in destination place but righteous soul livening destination place, so that wicked soul it don't problems after finishing macro concept world where to go,

But Righteous soul to wicked soul front line,

Wicked soul so wicked, so that wicked soul know that micro concept world is another destination place of "righteous soul living in destination place".

So then wicked souls with front line with righteous soul, then wicked soul see righteous soul how to live, righteous soul living is "it shares time with other, help other but also doing real love other", this is living with other, but also righteous soul living is "the poor & righteous soul" and "righteous soul& nothing", here is difference is soul with mind is not friend, wicked soul gradually know that, wicked soul try to distance from mind. Mind is getting much more than other.

Wicked soul know that righteous soul do not living in macro concept world, even in the macro concept world but still living in micro concept world of righteous soul living in destination living in destination place living.

Because righteous soul perfect distance from macro concept world mind, so that truly righteous soul living is on the micro cosmos of in the body, so that righteous soul living is truly living in righteous soul living in destination place living.

As then as the righteous soul front line with wicked soul

Wicked soul living with righteous soul then, righteous soul living behavior is really feel in excitement, just only one living "easy living excitement" is not compared with righteous soul living excitement of "it shares time with other, help other, but also doing real love other".

This is originality difference wicked soul friend with mind, but righteous soul enemy with mind, so that this is cause of righteous soul keep hearing broadcasting from righteous soul living in destination place, but wicked soul only depend on old knowledge so that, in the old knowledge all to be contaminated macro concept world mind so that, truly first a righteous soul hearing broadcasting but after time then macro concept world use in the macro concept world, so then, before creation of knowledge but plus mind of macro concept world being old knowledge so that wicked soul excitement with old knowledge because old knowledge is best to the wicked soul so that wicked soul win the game with others, wicked soul, wicked soul energy of "revenge and breaking is also winning energy of old knowledge memory or anyway wicked soul good at old knowledge getting", wicked soul adsorb old knowledge because wicked soul "easy living" is old knowledge is necessary.

But righteous soul creation of knowledge is perfect there is no mind only using running to the righteous soul living in destination place, so that righteous soul living running is keep coming problems, so then righteous all problems solving as creation of knowledge.

So that righteous soul living with wicked soul front line is

Wicked soul old knowledge to righteous soul creation of knowledge is mixed, so then here is wicked soul adsorb righteous soul creation of knowledge, then here is wicked soul getting know that righteous soul living world and wicked soul living world is not same.

Even in the same place in the macro concept world but wicked soul living and righteous soul living is not same is getting by wicked soul, so that wicked soul keep front line with righteous soul, until now wicked soul living is using "revenge and breaking energy using" easy living is best living, but righteous soul "doing real love" then living with other is best living is getting knowledge.

So then all of front line is creating

If do not build in the creating, then truly the time and space is fixed wicked soul to wicked soul, but righteous soul to be gradually being wicked soul so that, out of front line there is no righteous soul, but only macro concept world of mind livings and wicked soul livings are in the "easy living" then, the place there is no righteous soul.

Righteous soul living front line is

Only way to safe returning to the righteous soul living in destination place, so that righteous hard living is front line, this is righteous soul livings all necessary so that righteous soul living front line is macro concept world front line adopt, in the macro concept world all of actor to actor front line is created, then it must be front line is only to be me for other, in the case, me is not appeared but being for other circumstance, this is righteous soul front line.

Macro concept world front line will be being expanded front line to be.

Righteous soul front line with wicked soul then it must be "righteous soul is nothing"

Righteous soul front line with wicked soul, the sure of it, "righteous soul is nothing", and Righteous soul is to be being circumstance.

Righteous soul will live in "righteous soul & nothing"

Truly righteous soul to be being "righteous soul is being circumstance"

Because why righteous soul to be being circumstance is wicked soul energy of "revenge and breaking" so hard, so that righteous soul must be hidden from wicked soul "revenge and breaking" but also, here is wicked soul is variance of not true, wicked soul is think of wicked soul so that not true to true of righteous soul, then it also not true of past origin not rue true to be forgive by righteous soul, but think of wicked soul keep supplied to righteous soul, so then here is wicked soul is moving and variance but righteous soul of circumstance is true and eternity do not change, so that righteous soul to be being circumstance.

Truly micro concept world is righteous soul is just

Righteous soul of nothing living circumstance so that macro concept world of cosmos law in me is feel is righteous soul and nothing is this "nothing but feeling is circumstance"

Here is macro concept world front line is also

Righteous soul me front line wicked soul other, righteous soul to be humble and smile welcome wicked soul, then wicked soul feeling in excitement, in the front line righteous soul me energy of "doing real love is transfer to the wicked soul so that wicked soul feel in excitement"

In this wicked soul feeling is "nothing of righteous soul me but in the place excitement circumstance created" here is also wicked soul only here, because righteous soul to be being nothing. Here is Righteous soul front line to the wicked soul, so then front line with wicked soul who expect to be "easy living" even all of energy using "revenge and breaking", then righteous soul already harmony with circumstance so then, righteous soul is any problems to the wicked soul, so then in this time front line with wicked soul, righteous soul keep hearing broadcasting from righteous soul living in destination place, creating creation of knowledge.

Righteous soul to wicked soul front line is, to the righteous soul is opportunity righteous soul make known righteous soul living way, by doing real love wicked soul and help righteous soul living using creation of knowledge make know to the wicked soul.

But also wicked soul it is really important because wicked soul beginning in the front line with righteous soul, because wicked soul voyage in the macro concept world to be complete this turning macro concept world voyage how many do not know, this is wicked soul is urgent try to know creation of knowledge with righteous soul do real love wicked soul.

Between righteous soul and wicked soul front line is both urgent

Because front line is so precious important opportunity righteous soul is why voyage hard macro concept world, so then righteous soul mission is "meet a lover of wicked soul to create righteous soul and living with lover of righteous soul and safe returning macro concept world voyage", but also wicked soul is to be lover of righteous soul, so that wicked soul all save from wicked soul living, so that wicked soul to complete voyage of macro concept world, this is real urgent to the wicked soul.

Here is front line is

Wicked soul energy 50 + righteous soul energy 50 = 100, then here is wicked soul feel energy 100, righteous soul to be feel energy 100, so then, here is if living in righteous soul then, the righteous soul energy 100 used for wicked soul to be created to righteous soul, but also wicked soul energy is strong then wicked soul use energy 100.

But here is wicked soul energy 100 is variance in the front line is wicked soul get to know, that other 50 of righteous soul doing real love to the wicked soul then, here is righteous soul energy creation of knowledge with doing real love, so that wicked soul accept adsorb of righteous soul of creation of knowledge, then wicked soul solve problems using creation of knowledge, then here is wicked soul energy 100 is mixed with righteous soul then, here is righteous soul energy, so that in the front line wicked soul energy of righteous soul energy so that righteous soul living in destination place broadcasting is to be hear so, even time is required but wicked soul see, in the micro concept world there is other of righteous soul living in destination is clear.

As the righteous soul master of energy 100 is also support wicked soul energy 100, here is 50 is righteous soul so that here is in the front line, righteous soul energy 100 used for the creation of wicked soul to be righteous soul.

In the front line

Wicked soul energy is = wicked soul 50 + righteous soul 50 = here is wicked soul 100, if pure of wicked soul be living in the wicked soul, to be living in easy living

But here is Righteous soul mission is "righteous soul meet wicked soul of lover so then, righteous soul do real love wicked soul to create wicked soul to be righteous soul and safe come back to the righteous soul living in destination place" so that righteous soul is urgent do to mission clear.

In this front line righteous soul use righteous soul energy 100 for the wicked soul be creating righteous soul

In the front line wicked soul = wicked soul 50 + righteous soul +50 + Righteous soul doing real love wicked soul so then here is righteous soul energy 100 is added so, here is front line wicked to be create righteous soul then origin of righteous soul energy all help wicked soul.

Here is wicked soul to be create righteous soul

In the front line

Wicked soul energy 50 + righteous soul energy 50 = wicked soul energy 100 + Righteous soul energy 100 + helping righteous soul living in destination place energy = so then wicked soul energy only 50 but righteous soul energy is 150 + righteous soul living in destination place, so that wicked soul to be created to the righteous soul this is original righteous soul to be feel in excitement this is true and real hard but righteous soul mission clear.

Here is how to live in the macro concept world righteous soul

Righteous soul must live in "mind =1/ this is righteous soul is "the poor & righteous soul" growing to the righteous soul so that "righteous soul & nothing", this is keep going. To be that it needed energy of righteous soul so that righteous soul keep hearing broadcasting from righteous soul living destination place, but also doing righteous soul living behavior "it shares time with other, help other but also doing real love other".

Here is only me, righteous soul me living,

How to live is here make clear, in the macro concept world living of righteous soul living, righteous soul living is not secure or safe in the macro concept world living, most from micro to macro righteous soul living lost to the wicked soul "easy living", so that righteous soul living actor hard to see.

Here is righteous soul voyage is so fear of it, righteous soul to be living in the "mind=1/" "the poor & righteous soul" "righteous soul & nothing", but also righteous soul living behavior "it shares time with other, help other but also doing real love other" this is only living in righteous soul in the macro concept world.

"Righteous soul front line with wicked soul then it must be "righteous soul is nothing""

Righteous soul living front line with wicked soul is really hard but to be righteous soul living complete in the macro concept world, do real love wicked soul, that is only way to do real living in the macro concept world.

Micro concept world righteous soul me front line with wicked soul me, the macro concept world lover doing real love me, then here is wicked soul me feel huge in excitement

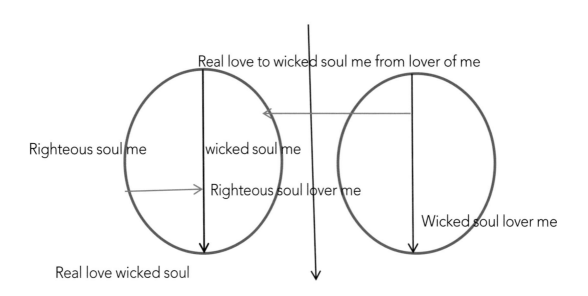

Real love to wicked soul me from lover of me

Righteous soul me   wicked soul me

Righteous soul lover me

Real love wicked soul   Wicked soul lover me

Micro concept world front line   **Macro concept world front line**

This is this book try to saying is all to be defined.

Micro concept world front line is Righteous soul do real love wicked soul me, so then here is front line is created.

Here of righteous soul me to wicked soul me front line is righteous soul me doing real love to wicked soul me, then here is righteous soul me is being circumstance to the wicked soul me, so that in the front line, righteous soul to be circumstance so that wicked soul me free and excitement of righteous soul me doing real love to the wicked soul with creation of knowledge.

Then here is micro concept world front line means that just only wicked soul me is this, while, then wicked soul feel is excitement because of righteous soul me doing real love, and then

Macro concept world front line to me

Here is other of lover try to do real love "ME", then here is lover of righteous soul do real love "ME" then in this time micro concept world front line righteous soul me to wicked soul me, so that righteous soul me is being in circumstance to the wicked soul, so that here in the micro concept me is now only excitement of wicked soul me is in me,

Then lover of righteous soul do real love "ME"

Here is macro concept world front line is create

Lover of righteous soul do real love me, then, "me" is now only excitement of wicked soul because of righteous soul is circumstance to the wicked soul me, so that directly wicked soul me adsorb of lover of righteous soul doing real love "me", so then "me is wicked soul" there for wicked soul adsorb lover of doing real love all get wicked soul me, so then wicked soul me feeling in huge excitement.

In this time macro concept world living me is really feeling is excitement.

There for wicked soul me feel excitement with righteous soul creation of knowledge also adsorb, so that wicked soul me getting being gradually changed into righteous soul me, here is so excitement change.

So that micro concept world front line

Macro concept world front line is keep continued this is necessary progress and change wicked soul me to change into righteous soul.

Righteous soul silent front line to wicked soul loudly

Righteous soul living in silent place, but wicked soul living at loudly place.

So then the living condition is difference so that righteous soul living in destination place is silent, but wicked soul living in destination place is loudly place.

Wicked soul living hard in the silent, but righteous soul living is not like in the loudly place.

So then righteous soul front line to the wicked soul so then, both hard front line, wicked soul try to be living in the loudly, but righteous soul to be hard with wicked soul condition, so then here is righteous soul front line so then, it must be righteous soul to be circumstance to the wicked soul loudly living.

Here is righteous soul has the excitement with just corner of "the poor & righteous soul" in the macro concept world, because righteous soul like silent place, but wicked soul try to do center of macro concept world because all of living center is loudly condition.

Truly

Here is wicked soul loudly living is made in "revenge and breaking" so then all of anger of living, so that wicked soul living with "think of wicked soul" but also all of saying and hearing is all not to be silent all energy using loudly voice.

But righteous soul

Try to do "it shares time with other, help other but also doing real love other" so that the righteous soul living is not any sound but also silent, do real living of righteous soul living is silent living, all the time righteous soul front line with other then, righteous soul living keep in silent living.

But also righteous soul living is hard and poor living so that righteous soul go with silent, righteous soul hear of broadcasting from righteous soul living in destination place, so then righteous soul follow the righteous soul broadcasting then, the living feeling in excitement this is real excitement because righteous soul keep a cosmos law, out of wicked soul revenge and breaking but righteous soul do living, as the righteous soul do like then sure of the wicked soul revenge righteous soul doing, this is feeling in the macro concept world righteous soul, in the sleeping time comes, wicked soul temptation to break cosmos law, but in the hard and poor time is righteous soul is clean clear from wicked soul revenge and breaking.

Righteous soul silent to wicked soul loudly front line

Here is righteous soul is only being wicked soul feeling of righteous soul of true and real love wicked soul, so that wicked soul feel righteous soul warm and silent and clean clear is feeling excitement to the wicked soul.

Righteous soul now living righteous soul living behavior of "it shares time with other, help other, but also doing real love other", so then this is righteous soul living front line wicked soul loudly living.

Wicked soul loudly living is energy consuming, so that as the wicked soul energy all used up, then righteous soul energy used for wicked soul, here is righteous soul mission carry, as the righteous soul energy used up then, wicked soul need to energy but energy is righteous soul living energy, this energy create in the "it shares time with other, help other but also doing real love other" so that, as the wicked soul adsorb righteous soul living energy then, wicked soul also feel righteous soul living energy, wicked soul gradually growing righteous soul living energy helping, but decreasing wicked soul living of consuming of loudly, but as the wicked soul keep adsorb righteous soul energy then, wicked soul also to be feel in silent living is excitement.

So long here is

Righteous soul silent front line to the wicked soul loudly is righteous soul living opportunity to mission carry, so that righteous soul do real love wicked soul of lover, then wicked soul of lover energy run out, so then, righteous soul do righteous soul living behavior to the wicked soul, this is also front line, so that "righteous soul shares time with wicked soul, and righteous soul help wicked soul but also doing real love wicked soul" so then wicked soul who is not out of energy, then wicked soul adsorb righteous soul living energy, this is wicked soul feel righteous soul energy then here is wicked soul know that righteous soul of creation of knowledge, but also wicked soul know that righteous soul living knowledge for the righteous soul living in destination place, but also righteous soul of creation of knowledge is cosmos law, so that wicked soul know that how to go for the macro concept world living completion.

Macro concept world living voyage complete is

Righteous soul keep running to the righteous soul living in destination place using righteous soul living energy, the same as wicked soul also dream as the wicked soul living energy sued up, then in the front with righteous soul so that wicked soul used righteous soul living energy so that wicked soul know that righteous soul use creation of knowledge, so that wicked soul knows how to macro concept world living voyage to safe and clear of macro concept world complete.

This is really important moment

Wicked soul know that righteous soul living is how important to macro concept world living.

If living wicked soul living, there is no answer to macro concept world completion living, this is really valuable and wicked soul creation to righteous soul beginning is happened to the wicked soul, this is great of righteous soul front line with wicked soul, then righteous soul do mission clear, this is also righteous soul macro concept world voyage mission carry out, then here is righteous soul to be changed into "righteous soul & nothing", this is righteous soul living in the macro concept world.

Righteous soul me here is feel miracle

Because righteous soul front line to the wicked soul, so that wicked soul to be create wicked soul to righteous soul, this is front line.

How hard both

Righteous soul also hard but also wicked soul also hard, because righteous soul hard wicked, but wicked also hard because wicked soul shift from wicked soul helping old knowledge to righteous soul of creation of knowledge, wicked soul feel fear, creation of knowledge is really possible fear of it, but creation of knowledge is true, so that wicked soul overcome of old knowledge "easy living" out of it, creation of new knowledge, hard living with other righteous soul living.

Wicked soul accept hard living, the poor and righteous soul living, but also wicked soul know that righteous soul's creation of knowledge but also righteous soul living energy by doing "it shares time with other, help other but also doing real love other", so that wicked soul know it, wicked soul out of "easy living", this is so hard but, accept so that wicked soul to be created as righteous soul living.

Righteous soul silent front line to the wicked soul loudly is now

Both "righteous soul" silent with create righteous soul silent so that righteous soul mission clear, this is really excitement with create righteous soul in silent.

Righteous soul front line to the wicked soul is warm and peace of wicked soul circumstance

Righteous soul create front line to the wicked soul

Righteous soul all use for the wicked soul front line

Righteous soul now in the "righteous soul & nothing"

Righteous soul "doing real love"

Righteous soul "creation of knowledge"

Righteous soul "energy" do not consuming but only use runs for the righteous soul living in destination place

Righteous soul living in silent and clean clear living

Righteous soul behavior "it shares time with wicked soul and help wicked soul and but also doing real love other"

These righteous soul living tools all mixed to create front line to the wicked soul

So that in the righteous soul front line, wicked soul feeling is so comfortable, peace and really excitement furthermore get knowledge of creation of knowledge.

Wicked soul feels a new and really safe and strange feeling,

Then wicked soul living conditions is old knowledge using

Wicked soul living by "revenge and breaking" energy using

Wicked soul loudly and dirty living

Wicked soul energy using "easy living"

In the righteous soul front line

Wicked soul feels in not in easy living but in excitement but also old knowledge changed into creation of knowledge.

In the righteous soul front line wicked soul is all used righteous soul living tools, so that wicked soul uses creation of knowledge, while wicked soul knows that macro concept world living complete living ways.

Here in the righteous soul living front line, wicked soul also use righteous soul living, so that even wicked soul is not in now righteous soul, but righteous soul front line is all help wicked soul, so that by helping wicked soul, righteous soul living in the same as other righteous soul livings.

Truly

Here righteous soul living front line comfortable and peace and excitement with creation of knowledge then, here is wicked soul to be righteous soul, then wicked soul is before creating a material, so that wicked soul is so weak in the righteous soul living,

But before wicked soul so huge energy but the "revenge and breaking" energy wicked soul now in the righteous soul creature of front line, so then wicked soul here is all support righteous soul living tools then, wicked soul to be righteous soul then here all righteous souls are all adult, but wicked to be righteous soul then it is infant of righteous soul, this is wicked soul to be creating of righteous soul, then here is wicked soul to righteous soul, then an infant of righteous soul, so that here is righteous soul creating front line is all to be creator role.

In the front line

Wicked soul gradually changed into creation of righteous soul, so then righteous energy used for the wicked soul creating righteous soul, this is all of effort.

Why righteous soul hard in the macro concept world is righteous soul front line to the wicked soul then, wicked soul to be created to the righteous soul

This is so hard

But all of righteous souls are hard living in the macro concept world because

Macro concept world wicked souls huge numbers, so that righteous soul living is miracle.

But here is a righteous soul create front line to the wicked soul then here is really righteous soul do living in righteous soul living.

So then, in the righteous soul front line

Keep continued front line with wicked soul, so then truly righteous soul is also really excitement but also here righteous soul feel "thank to the creator in the righteous soul living in destination place", at now here macro concept world righteous soul feel that, so righteous soul consistent doing "righteous soul time use for wicked soul, and help wicked soul but also all of doing real love to wicked soul" this is keep doing complete create from wicked soul to righteous soul.

In this time

Wicked soul feel that strong wicked soul changed to infant of righteous soul, so that this change is all forgive from creator cosmos law, so that wicked soul to be righteous soul, then all of past orientated sinful, and wicked soul energy all to be used up, while in the front line of righteous soul, wicked soul all used up of wicked soul energy, but to living energy required then here is front line, helped by righteous soul, so that wicked soul living energy used righteous soul living energy, so that while righteous soul energy using automatically creation of knowledge also getting, so that wicked soul old knowledge gradually disappeared to the wicked soul, in the end righteous soul of creation of knowledge occupied in the wicked soul, so then wicked soul getting know that, how to complete macro concept world voyage complete.

The way is only this way, if in this front line if not to be changed into creating righteous soul then, keep incomplete macro concept world, this is really urgent chance to me to live in righteous soul, this is helping by creation of knowledge with real love, this is really urgent do real love to the righteous soul, because righteous soul do real love lover, so that righteous soul create lover of wicked soul, the really best of best living place righteous soul living in destination place carry righteous soul of wicked soul, but to go for the righteous soul living in destination place, only righteous soul, so that righteous soul all effort to create righteous soul, so then, here is also righteous soul is urgent, so righteous soul all of energy all of doing real love, and all of creation of knowledge, supply because how hard to the wicked soul, because wicked soul all adult soul of wicked soul to now infant of righteous soul, this is changed from changed wicked soul to righteous soul.

This is disappeared to wicked soul, but created to righteous soul, then, this process is so hard to the wicked soul also, it must be wicked soul so fear of out of wicked soul easy living, but wicked soul all do by lover of righteous soul, so that in the righteous soul front line, wicked soul to be righteous soul infant, so then here is righteous soul creating righteous soul to be real baby of creation of knowledge.

Then here is righteous soul front line of righteous soul really dong real love created a new righteous soul to be helped and keep with righteous soul helping righteous soul, here is macro concept world, righteous soul keep "righteous soul shares time with baby of righteous soul and help baby of righteous soul, but also doing real love baby of righteous soul.

Here is great creation of knowledge is comes to me

Macro concept world righteous soul living is do real love lover of wicked soul, this is then righteous soul do like righteous soul of infant, do love that, this is real love, as the righteous soul front line righteous soul create wicked soul to righteous soul, this is truly righteous soul macro concept world living.

Righteous soul in the macro concept world front line is

At now perfectly wicked soul to be righteous soul, but created righteous soul is so weak in energy so that keep righteous soul doing righteous soul living behavior in the macro concept world, then so that righteous soul helping beginning righteous soul of "the poor & righteous soul" keep growing to "righteous soul & nothing", then in the end same with now like righteous soul me, at now righteous soul souls same at last a creation of righteous soul to be adult righteous soul, then righteous soul me and create righteous soul of lover to be living in the macro concept world living in excitement and both lover of righteous souls will safe comeback to the righteous soul living in destination place.

Wicked soul front line to righteous soul

Wicked soul front line to the righteous soul

Wicked soul use "revenge and breaking" for only wicked soul living easy living, righteous soul so hard with in the wicked soul front line.

Here is wicked soul combined with macro concept world mind, so that wicked soul front line is righteous soul disappearing is easily possible.

Then here is wicked soul plus mind is "wicked soul easy living" plus mind "getting much more than other" is strong endless mind, so that righteous soul living condition is mind is 1/limitless about to mind to zero is righteous soul basic living condition, but here is wicked soul revenge and breaking energy then, righteous soul living so hard, in the end disappeared.

Then

Righteous soul disappeared but now appeared up of wicked soul, so then here is righteous soul disappear, this is righteous soul living in destination place so miss, in the macro concept world wicked soul energy also huge but also macro concept world mind is also limitless, then how to righteous soul can be living in the huge hard living condition.

So long here is righteous soul so easily changed into wicked soul, then here is all loss, but also wicked soul, mind getting space, it is hard to take back of righteous soul, then this is a role of righteous soul, role player disappeared then, in the place righteous soul living in destination place ordained work, can't doing so that, all of difference, expected planning difference is happened.

So that righteous soul living in destination place to be estimate that, a righteous soul failed running to the righteous soul living voyage orbit, so that righteous soul living in destination broadcasting do not hear, then righteous soul living in destination broadcasting all forgotten.

Wicked soul front line to the righteous soul

This is wicked soul all living on the old knowledge so that righteous soul do not solve the problems to the righteous soul living in destination place, so that righteous soul runs to the voyage obit, closed.

At now so hard

But also as the same time, mind is opportunity so long in the righteous soul disappeared then mind getting with body.

So then here is possible mind level living actor and wicked soul living actor comes.

Wicked soul and mind living actor is even same condition of energy consuming living so that to fill consumed energy so that mind and wicked soul try to get much more than other, so that mind get much more than other, but also wicked soul help mind to get it, so that mind and wicked soul so harmony, but mind living do not stop because all of getting much more than other is really good well.

So that mind is keep increasing getting, then here is wicked soul is "revenge and breaking" so long here is micro concept world wicked soul react, mind getting all of energy do revenged and breaking mind, so that mind to be dreamed to be happy with full of energy, then in a moment there is no happy but there is wicked soul "easy living".

Wicked soul "easy living" is originality wicked soul only living easy so long wicked soul "easy living" is only one, but here is righteous soul living is "it shares time with other, help other but also doing real love other"

Wicked soul only one, but righteous soul with other,

So long a righteous soul living disappeared then, around of before righteous soul, to be frill wicked soul, so that there is no righteous soul living "excitement", all to be living in hard living.

Here is very change is wicked soul livings all use old knowledge so that mind and wicked souls are all living wicked soul knowledge, but also there is no creation of knowledge from righteous soul living in destination place, then wicked soul and mind living place living at the past orientations.

Wicked souls are all living only wicked soul living "easy living" so that wicked soul believe that old knowledge so that they are all to be living well compared with mind is so hard living, because mind do not know, even old knowledge so that wicked soul get a power to live on the time and space, but mind living is getting harder, because there is not increased but same energy all used up by the wicked soul.

How to do?

Wicked soul front line to wicked soul

Wicked soul combined to mind so that huge strong "revenge and breaking" righteous soul is so easy, so then righteous souls all to be easily changed into wicked soul, truly in the macro concept world wicked soul living is easy than living in righteous soul, because it don't feel responsibility the living condition deteriorate as the all to be increased wicked soul, then just only living in wicked soul living "easy living" so that there is no just like righteous soul of creation of knowledge so that mind levels livings are all to be salver of wicked souls.

But while a righteous soul survive and righteous soul front line to the wicked soul then, righteous soul save form wicked soul righteous soul, so then righteous behavior of "it shared time with other, help other but also doing real love other", here is righteous soul living is how help mind level livings, but also as the righteous soul living then, there is no mind level livings not to be salver of righteous soul living, but if living wicked soul then, this is based on old knowledge so that there is no creation of energy so that, all of mind level livings are to be salver to the wicked souls.

So why righteous soul livings survive is important is here

But this is all start all of livings from me but other]

If I living in righteous soul then, righteous soul living is possible, but if righteous soul me disappeared then truly, living me is wicked soul, this living is salver living.

Here is why righteous soul front line is urgent is this

Righteous soul front line to the wicked soul is, even save wicked soul, but also survive in the front line is urgent.

Righteous soul living tools is "doing real love" but if do not do "doing real love" then, righteous soul living how to live in the righteous soul living.

But also righteous soul living is only hearing righteous soul living broadcasting and getting creation of knowledge to survive to the wicked soul old knowledge.

How to live here?

In this macro concept world how to live is living?

Truly real living is righteous soul, so then real living of righteous soul if do not do real love wicked soul then, wicked soul will anger but also "revenge and breaking", then here is righteous soul all to be disappeared.

Whose responsibility hard to righteous soul livings then

All is from me,

If living on the old knowledge then, righteous soul me out of old knowledge this is really important, creation of knowledge is hearing broadcasting then, how to live is getting, so that righteous soul living is must be

Righteous soul living of creation of knowledge so that width is 1/, dept is, so long

$1/x = 1/$, here is macro concept world reality is width, then truly in the macro concept world width is about to zero, even not zero, so that it must be $0x = 0$, here is not zero

This is righteous soul living, here is righteous soul living depend on creation of knowledge then here is width is 1/, this means that righteous soul living in the macro concept world do not do other make hard but righteous soul living is creation of knowledge so that, wicked soul old knowledge time there is no energy creating but righteous soul living on the creation of knowledge then, expand energy, so called energy is + righteous soul creation of energy.

So that while righteous soul livings

Then there is no mind not to be salver of righteous soul livings

But if wicked soul living s place

Wicked soul living place width is **x**depth 1/ = 1 here is only 1 is this is old knowledge time, there is no increased, but also old knowledge make hard others, for the wicked soul easy living then, wicked soul used "revenge and breaking energy" so that all of mind levels are to be salver of wicked souls

But also wicked soul old knowledge is strong power so that if do not go through old knowledge mind level living is hard to live, on, but all of mind try to be like living of wicked soul old knowledge of "easy living" but there is no creative knowledge so that all of mind livings are to be slaver of wicked soul livings.

This is really important how to live in me

If living me as the righteous soul living then

Righteous soul living neighbors are all to be living in excitement, but if I live in the wicked soul then all of my neighbors are to be my salvers.

Which way living?

Righteous soul living of "it shares time with other, help other but also doing real love other"

But living in wicked soul only living easy living me?

Which is better?

Truly all of livings structure is

"From micro concept world of wicked soul and righteous soul + from macro concept world of mind with body"

This is all same

But who live in wicked soul living

Who lives in the mind level living?

Who is living in the righteous soul living?

This answer is to live righteous soul living is itself is make no other to be living salver, but if do not living righteous soul then automatically other of mind level livings are to be salver so that this macro concept world living righteous soul living is only real living.

Righteous soul urgent must do live keep every moment do live in the "doing real love wicked soul" then righteous soul living not to be disappeared.

Righteous soul front line of "there is no mind, there is no me"

Righteous soul front line is wicked soul to be change from wicked soul to righteous soul.

So that Righteous soul front line to the wicked soul is Righteous soul is being circumstance.

But macro concept world me is keep recite "there is no mind, there is no me", this is same as in the micro concept world right soul being circumstance for wicked soul, but also macro concept world me is do "there is no mind, there is no me", actually in the macro concept world is major living structure is mind, so then as there is no mind, then mindful me is not in the macro concept but truly micro concept world as mind to be zero then righteous soul living is string activation.

So long, righteous soul, and righteous soul me is all the time being circumstance in the front line, because if there is" there is mind and there is me" then front line with other, in the macro concept world, then here is front line is to be macro concept world huge dispute, because here is conflict between strong "revenge and breaking energy of wicked soul" to Righteous soul me, then righteous soul must be doing not role of righteous soul "doing real love other".

Here is same in the micro concept world

If I see in me, in the time of meditation but also keep watching then, in me, just righteous soul, there is no move but being circumstance for wicked soul, so then wicked soul to be free, doing not care of righteous soul, the same as in the macro concept world "there is no mind, there is no me", then in the macro concept world me living with me, then the wicked soul me living free, but as there is no mind, there is no me, then wicked soul me in the macro concept world, free and do living in wicked soul, but the wicked soul feel in excitement with righteous soul me.

Righteous soul is do not see, Righteous soul me is also do not see, this is righteous soul & nothing, just seen righteous soul is not see but the same as in the macro concept world of seen world "body", so that in the macro concept world body is major, so that do not know righteous soul, wicked soul living.

Righteous soul front line to the wicked soul is righteous soul mission in the macro concept world voyage, so that Righteous soul front line to wicked soul, here is righteous soul has the righteous soul mission, this is really macro concept world also important creation of knowledge, just front line is enemy to enemy so then, even in the micro concept world righteous soul living in destination place and wicked soul living in destination is not mixed.

But macro concept world righteous soul and wicked soul living in the front line, then here is righteous soul is being circumstance for the wicked soul, as see or feel micro concept world then righteous soul is living in the silent of clean clear, the here is space, so then here is there is nothing, but feel a moving and change wicked soul, here is connect to "think of wicked soul" so then in the wicked soul move then, just seeing of righteous soul is feeling that being circumstance for the wicked soul as the front line.

Here is righteous soul front line with wicked soul then, righteous soul keep doing righteous soul living behavior "it shares time with wicked soul, help wicked to learn creation of knowledge, but also righteous soul do real love wicked soul", this behavior is not hurry, constantly "righteous soul shares time with wicked soul, help wicked soul to lean creation of knowledge, and doing real love wicked soul".

As the righteous soul do constantly living of righteous soul, so that wicked soul huge "revenge and breaking energy" defend macro concept world me to be damaged from wicked soul.

Wicked soul has the "revenge and breaking energy" this is keep supply to me of "old knowledge includes ordering to macro concept me to revenge and breaking includes me and other.

Here is righteous soul and wicked soul front line, then righteous soul is really important, if righteous soul is so weak then, wicked soul "revenge and breaking energy" who depend, so to be offend macro concept me, but also wicked soul use macro concept me wicked soul living in destination place warrior of "revenge and breaking" of macro concept world and micro concept world righteous soul, so that as righteous soul living front line is really important.

Righteous soul to wicked soul front line is

Strong valance righteous soul to wicked soul, if this valance is breaking, then macro concept world to be damaged, then righteous soul front line is so constantly " it shares time with wicked soul help wicked soul, and doing real love wicked soul"

Righteous soul keeps doing this for macro concept world living whole

Because why here is righteous soul first to survive but also, to be survive then, wicked soul must be not to be used "revenge and breaking" so that righteous soul keep "it shares time with wicked soul and help wicked soul but also doing real love wicked soul", this behavior is righteous soul living in the macro concept world major.

So then, doing real love is

"Righteous soul do real love to the wicked soul" this is defined of righteous soul doing real love.

Righteous soul doing real love wicked soul is surviving righteous soul oneself, if in the macro concept world righteous soul living actor do not do real love wicked soul, then at first damaged from must do real love of wicked soul so then, as the righteous soul do not do constant love wicked soul, then the wicked soul first damage righteous soul me, but also do not do real love then, the righteous soul almost to be disappeared from righteous soul living voyage orbit.

Righteous soul front line to wicked soul, in this fear of living is righteous soul living in the voyage in the macro concept world is the living is "the poor & righteous soul; this living is all of hard living and there is no mind, here is so that the poor and righteous soul is just living righteous soul, so then the living is so hard living, so that righteous soul living in destination place righteous soul creating all to be being disappeared, so in the righteous soul living in destination keep creating righteous soul.

Righteous soul front line to wicked soul, then righteous soul must be "there is no mind, there is no me", this is real to do solution of creation of knowledge.

In the living of macro concept world

How to live with others in the macro concept world

In this macro concept world

Wicked soul, mind level livings, but also righteous soul, here is righteous soul living actor keep voyage righteous soul living macro concept world, but also righteous soul living with wicked soul and mind level livings, in the macro concept world so then, righteous soul living is macro concept living with micro concept world voyage living coincidently same living.

So then

Righteous soul keep hearing broadcasting from righteous soul living in destination place, so that righteous soul move and runs for the righteous soul living in destination place, so long all to be optimistic getting but also the living is righteous soul living energy getting "it shares time with other, help other but also doing real love other" this is cause of righteous soul living energy getting.

So that

Righteous soul living macro concept world living then the way is "there is no mind, and there is no me"

But righteous soul doing micro concept world living is "it shares time with other and help other and doing real love other" this two livings is righteous soul

So then righteous soul front line with wicked soul is also constant living "righteous soul constant do real love wicked soul so then in me, wicked soul to be created as the righteous soul then, the front line is disappeared, then automatically micro concept world me is righteous soul living.

Then time is up, macro concept world living voyage to be end then righteous soul living in destination place beginning then, the righteous soul living actor automatically safe returning to the righteous soul living in destination place.

In the macro concept world righteous soul is constant do righteous soul living behavior to the wicked soul "righteous soul shares time with wicked soul, and help wicked soul to learn creation of knowledge from righteous soul living in destination place but also do real love wicked soul" this is righteous soul living constant living.

This living is also righteous soul to righteous soul living.

Righteous soul living in the macro concept world living is also "there is no mind, there is no me" then, others living in me, all to be feel in excitement, because there is no me, so that righteous soul me fully all of righteous soul living energy for the wicked souls.

Macro concept world living righteous soul feel "there is no mind, there is no me", this is only living in the macro concept world living.

But also righteous soul living in the macro concept world is "it shares time with other, help other but also doing real love other"

These both macro concept world living, micro concept world voyage living both righteous soul living.

Then safe and returning to the righteous soul living in destination place meet righteous soul me creator of righteous soul, as righteous soul me safe returning to the righteous soul living in destination place them how to be feel in excitement meet righteous soul me creator this is

Really excitement and living in righteous soul living in destination place to the eternity.

Righteous soul sees in the front line to the wicked soul

Righteous soul front line with wicked soul

Righteous soul excitement doing real love wicked soul, who is to be righteous soul living.

Righteous soul sees wicked soul of lover.

To the righteous soul must be creating wicked soul to righteous soul, this is mission so that righteous soul really excitement, at now create front line,

Righteous soul me living in the macro concept world is how hard to survive from strong energy of "revenge and breaking" wicked soul, so that righteous soul living has been "the poor & righteous soul".

But now righteous soul growing, then righteous soul create front line with wicked soul so then right now righteous soul is in "righteous soul & nothing", righteous soul come to reach at the from the poor & righteous soul to now in the righteous soul and nothing.

Righteous soul living of "righteous soul & nothing", this is now living is beyond of wicked soul livings worlds so that righteous soul & nothing is create righteous soul front line, here is "righteous soul & nothing" is "nothing" so then righteous soul is not to be seen to the wicked soul, but wicked soul feel of righteous soul, so that wicked soul "revenge and breaking energy is not effect to the righteous soul& nothing".

Righteous soul & nothing to the wicked soul then, how to be feature, then "righteous soul & nothing created for the wicked soul, so that it must be wicked soul to be in the righteous soul & nothing, so then, here is righteous soul is to be wicked soul to be righteous soul, all do in the nearest do righteous soul living behavior " righteous soul shares time with wicked soul, help wicked soul to hear of creation of knowledge, and righteous soul do real love wicked soul"

Righteous soul sees in the front line to the wicked soul

"Righteous soul & nothing" do real love wicked soul then, righteous soul feel really doing real love to the wicked soul, so that righteous soul try to save from wicked soul to righteous soul, righteous soul knows that how hard living in the wicked soul living in destination place, so that the lover of wicked soul to be created by righteous soul.

Righteous soul is now in the macro concept world to be creator of wicked soul to be righteous soul, so then how hard, the creator hard living but righteous soul do accept in excitement because now living in wicked soul but if do create wicked soul then, a new create righteous soul also know that doing real love so then, as the creating righteous soul do real love already planned to meet both lovers to be feel in excitement because doing real love each other's.

Righteous soul see to be created wicked soul of lover, then righteous soul meet a wicked soul of lover who seek in the macro concept world, so righteous soul feel excitement, because it is beginning to be mission clear; mission is "righteous soul meet wicked soul of lover then righteous soul create lover of wicked soul to be living in righteous soul, then to be safe returning to the righteous soul living in destination place.

At now in the macro concept world so hard with love of wicked soul, but righteous soul me help living of "creation of knowledge", but to be wicked soul of lover stick to depend on old knowledge but endless help to learn creation of knowledge from righteous soul living in destination place, some of hear but soon help to lover of wicked soul, then wicked soul of lover to be learning that wicked soul do not know, righteous soul living in destination place but to know that, so that righteous soul & nothing, a wicked soul of lover to see righteous soul me can see but wicked soul do not effect "revenge and breaking" because righteous soul is now in the "righteous soul & nothing".

Here is Righteous soul & nothing doing real love wicked soul is string huge effective to the wicked soul, how to wicked soul to create a new of righteous soul, this is huge and endless righteous soul living energy.

It must be righteous soul all of righteous soul energy uses for the wicked soul of lover to be created righteous soul

Righteous soul living is

"the poor & righteous soul" it grows to the "righteous soul & nothing" this process how hard how many time temptation from wicked soul "easy living" and mind level "getting much more than other", these all of temptation and hard living and now to "righteous soul & nothing".

"Righteous soul & nothing" doing real love other is happening in the righteous soul front line to the wicked soul of lover.

This is righteous soul living is important because as the righteous soul survive to the righteous soul & nothing then, righteous soul doing real love, this energy is much more than mightier of wicked soul revenge and breaking energy, this energy was fear to the "poor & righteous soul" but now "righteous soul & nothing" is huge energy so that wicked soul energy all covering by the righteous soul and nothing of doing real love wicked soul.

So that as the righteous soul and nothing feels excitement, because righteous soul create front line righteous soul can do all to create from wicked soul to righteous soul, this is righteous soul feel really excitement, because to the righteous soul, create wicked soul is, strong of adult of wicked soul to be baby of righteous soul so that, righteous soul & nothing of doing real love infant of a new righteous soul must be helped by righteous soul, so then, righteous soul time all share with new created righteous soul, this is righteous soul & nothing's real excitement living.

Seong Ju Choi

This is righteous soul living sees lover of wicked soul then, lover of infant of righteous soul, this is really excitement, so long here of macro concept world righteous soul living is save a wicked soul to righteous soul this is righteous soul real living.

A righteous soul living is true and creation of knowledge, so then this is all of righteous soul do live just micro concept world living like, so that just second of time is all attentive to the righteous soul living, this is create righteous soul's front line to the wicked soul.

This is righteous soul mission is now doing. This is really feels in excitement, righteous soul feeling is excitement.

Righteous soul front line is

Righteous soul is circumstance

Righteous soul is "here is but to be righteous soul & nothing"

But wicked soul is keep varying anger, hard revenge and breaking behavior.

Righteous soul front line is wicked soul moving feeling sad and excitement all is changed in the circumstance of righteous soul &nothing.

So that righteous soul keep warm and feeling good to the wicked soul, here also righteous soul endless doing righteous soul behavior "righteous soul shares time with wicked soul and righteous soul helping wicked soul to be learn of righteous soul living knowledge of creation of knowledge but also righteous soul doing real love wicked soul.

Then in the righteous soul to wicked soul front line wicked soul feels in excitement but also wicked soul accepts righteous soul doing real love with creation of knowledge.

But righteous soul also happened doing front line

Then wicked soul do not feel in excitement, so that here is righteous soul is here or not then in the front line feeling is feeling but there is no righteous soul in the circumstance of righteous soul & nothing then, in the circumstance is cold and lonesome so that wicked soul feel sorrowful, righteous soul living doing real love wicked soul is wicked soul living feeling is not in sorrowful.

So then in this righteous soul front line is wicked soul living feeing direct connection, so that righteous soul and wicked soul is also must string front line, if both front line is keeping then, here is righteous soul living string or not then, wicked soul living to be living in excitement or not, but otherwise

In the front line wicked soul to righteous soul then,

Righteous soul all to be disappeared then, in the front line is wicked soul variance and just moving to the righteous soul, then righteous soul to be loss of righteous soul living, so then the wicked soul front line must be all occupied in wicked soul moving, so that in the micro concept world living all loudly and dirty all of past living residue of garbage filling.

So long wicked soul of past orientation of old knowledge and revenge and breaking energy then with all of residue of past livings so that, automatically wicked soul string but righteous soul would be disappeared.

Then the macro concept world feeling then the wicked soul living is all governing by the past residue of "thinking of wicked soul", these thinking is all old knowledge, it never expected thinking of residue of garbage is getting out in the macro concept world then the wicked soul living behavior is all macro concept world to be out of order.

So then righteous soul front line is huge important

Righteous soul front line to the wicked soul is

This front line is righteous soul mission "righteous souls meets wicked soul of lover and create righteous soul and safe comeback to the righteous soul living in destination place"

So then righteous soul front line is also micro concept world so called in "me" righteous soul front line but also in the macro concept world front line is living, here is macro concept world front line is based on the "there is no mind, there is no me" but also, truly righteous soul & nothing of macro concept world living.

Righteous soul living front line is all to be wicked soul righteous soul creating, so does, in the righteous soul front line with wicked soul, righteous soul helping learning to creation of knowledge with doing real love is all to create righteous soul, so then in the micro concept world, just like

01234567890, here is first "0" is micro concept world to macro concept world, so that here is "0" righteous soul meet wicked soul, then here is wicked soul living is "revenge and breaking, righteous soul is "doing real love" so all anti character how hard righteous soul living but righteous soul must do righteous soul to wicked soul front line, this is righteous soul to be living in the macro concept world or not is critical living this is first "0", so that righteous soul do real love wicked soul, but also to the wicked soul, righteous soul living creation of knowledge also helping to learn, but also wicked soul also change to living is righteous soul, then the living is only macro concept world complete living, but also not anymore to be fallen to the wicked soul, but also you can living in the righteous soul in the macro concept world then, wicked soul you also like me living in righteous soul.

If righteous soul front line to wicked soul

Then in the front line righteous soul living behavior of "righteous soul shares time with wicked soul, and helping to learn creation of knowledge, but also doing real love wicked soul" then what happen to righteous soul survive in the first "0", but also then righteous soul to be living in the macro concept world "the poor & righteous soul", this is righteous soul living.

Righteous soul front line to wicked soul

Then, even keep living with wicked soul, but "the poor & righteous soul" then in the front line, as using "doing real love wicked soul" then both are survive or righteous soul and wicked soul to be created to righteous soul, then it must be infer that macro concept living of strong righteous soul living, if this then, in the macro concept world place all to be influenced of righteous soul living.

Righteous soul front line to wicked soul

This is must be front time, then wicked soul living energy is strong, then righteous soul hurry not to be used wicked soul living "revenge and breaking energy", so called this is urgent to the righteous soul livings but as the time flows then, gradually righteous soul do righteous soul living behavior "it shares time with other, help other but also doing real love other".

So long wicked soul accept gradually as both doing real love with creation of knowledge, so that wicked soul do not used solving living problems by creation of knowledge, then learning how to live but also wicked soul feel and know that old knowledge do not solve now living problems but righteous soul creation of knowledge is can solve the problems so then wicked soul keep using righteous soul and adsorb righteous soul doing real love.

In the creation of knowledge is truly righteous soul runs to the righteous soul living in destination place going problems solving, so then, as wicked soul use creation of knowledge then wicked soul knows that how to live is like righteous soul living to the end of macro concept world then safe complete living, so that wicked soul getting knows how to live is complete living in the macro concept world.

So then, righteous soul front line to the wicked soul

Then this is really feel in excitement, because righteous soul living clear of survive righteous soul living but also wicked soul to be creating righteous soul, so that righteous soul living feeling is so excitement but also, here is righteous soul living in destination place all of helping now living in the front line to the wicked soul, then righteous soul all helping front line in righteous soul.

Righteous soul front line to wicked soul

This is first righteous soul survive

Second is helping wicked soul be creating righteous soul

Finally righteous soul create wicked soul to creation of righteous soul then righteous soul from wicked soul to righteous soul infant of baby all real love of bringing up now so that righteous soul living doing real love lover of wicked soul, is how love lover, this living is in the righteous soul living in destination place huge love lover, then how you know, just like feel creator of lover to wicked soul created righteous soul, then the lover of creating righteous soul do real love as the righteous soul, then righteous soul feeling in huge excitement.

Righteous soul front line is

Ultimate creating wicked soul lover to righteous soul, then created righteous soul do real love to righteous soul, so that micro concept world righteous soul living in destination place to seek in the macro concept world, so that the dangerous voyage start, but as the righteous soul front line, so that meet wicked soul but the wicked soul created by the righteous soul, so that righteous soul creator in the front lie a wicked soul of lover so that creator of righteous soul creating of righteous soul relationship is huge strong this is eternity living in the righteous soul living in destination place.

Righteous soul front line energy is 100

Righteous soul front line to wicked soul, then righteous soul energy is 100.

Righteous soul is only using "doing real love"

Wicked soul use "revenge and breaking"

Why righteous soul do create front line to the wicked soul

The answer is to macro concept world voyage mission carry

The mission is "meet lover of wicked soul then create lover of wicked soul to righteous soul, and created righteous soul and righteous both safe returning to the righteous soul living in destination place.

The how righteous soul does in the front line

Righteous soul energy is 100

In the front line of righteous soul to wicked soul then

Righteous soul feel fear of being disappeared cause of wicked soul "revenge and breaking" so that righteous soul keep surviving so that it required to from wicked soul energy 50

But also righteous soul try to create wicked soul to righteous soul so that righteous soul creating energy of cause of righteous soul energy 50

So that in the righteous soul front line to wicked soul,

Righteous soul energy is

Righteous soul feel fear of being disappeared cause of wicked soul "revenge and breaking" so that righteous soul keep surviving so that it required to from wicked soul energy 50

+

Righteous soul try to create wicked soul to righteous soul so that righteous soul creating energy of cause of righteous soul energy 50

= in the front line righteous soul energy 100

So that righteous soul survives in the front line and keep doing real love wicked soul to end of creating wicked soul righteous soul.

Why righteous soul create front line to the wicked soul

This is righteous soul save living wicked soul, so that righteous soul took compassion on the lover of wicked soul this is doing real love, so that righteous soul do real love wicked soul.

But also

In the macro concept world mission is originality living in the micro concept world righteous soul living in destination place living in excitement with the lover eternity.

So that righteous soul do create front line to the wicked soul, this is righteous soul doing real love.

Righteous soul doing real love to the wicked soul then here is helping to learn of righteous soul living ways of creation of knowledge.

"Righteous soul front line energy is 100"

Righteous soul living is also every moment runs to the righteous soul living destination place, hearing broadcasting from righteous soul living in destination place, that is creation of knowledge.

So then in the front line to the wicked soul

Righteous soul energy is

Cause of wicked soul energy 50 + cause of righteous soul energy 50 + creation of knowledge and as running to the righteous soul, so then other righteous souls helping righteous soul me running to the righteous soul living in destination place.

So that righteous soul create front line to the wicked soul

Even how hard lover of wicked soul but righteous soul doing real love to the wicked soul is mightier than wicked soul "revenge and breaking".

Already has living in the macro concept world, all of safe returning to the righteous souls all knows how hard with in the front line with lover of wicked soul, but safe returned righteous souls, so that righteous soul in the righteous soul living in destination place do helping now living in the macro concept world.

So that in the front line of macro concept world

Is also righteous soul living in destination place, but just in the front line is only wicked soul, so that righteous soul front line righteous soul doing only "doing real love" then righteous soul does create wicked soul to be righteous soul.

Righteous soul in the macro concept world

In the front line all living for lover of wicked soul to be righteous soul as the righteous soul energy 100 using, this is righteous soul living it is.

Righteous soul front line of circumstance

Righteous soul is in the front line of circumstance

Righteous soul is space of clean clear silent

But here living and moving is wicked souls.

Righteous soul feels that noisy wicked soul cry, calculate and todays doing something also all living of wicked soul living place.

Righteous soul front line of circumstance is wicked soul all do, do not want to do, reluctance to do, anger, be irritated all of behaviors etc.

So that doing wicked soul living behavior but all know that as the space and silent clean clear, so that righteous soul do front line warm and comfort to the wicked souls, so that wicked souls are not anger and agitate in it.

As the righteous soul do front line with comfort and warm in it, so that wicked soul do not use "revenge and breaking energy" then, here is righteous feel of silent and clean clear is broken.

Just Righteous soul do being circumstance so then, righteous soul to be clean clear and even much more than harmony with other circumstance then wicked soul living easy feeling.

Wicked soul living like to be living in "easy living", so that righteous soul create front line for the wicked soul easy, but here is righteous soul also help learning of "it shares time with other, help other but also doing real love other"

Because why righteous soul do help wicked soul to learn creation of knowledge, this is righteous soul living knowledge, why righteous soul create front line to the wicked soul, it is righteous soul to be being righteous soul living.

So that here is righteous soul front line is to the wicked soul feel warm and comfortable then wicked soul governed by the righteous soul not to be do "revenge and breaking".

Righteous soul front line circumstance

Is harmony with around of circumstance so that righteous soul front line to the wicked soul is like righteous soul livening in destination place, righteous soul already know, because in the created at the righteous soul living in destination place, how comfortable and excitement but also the place warm place, so that now righteous soul front line to the wicked soul, then wicked to live at the righteous soul front lime, the same as wicked soul is much more than brilliants, in the righteous soul front line to the wicked soul, then if wicked soul feel in the front line easy living feeling, but wicked soul do not feel in easy living feeling then, wicked soul do not living at the righteous soul front line, then righteous soul do not governing wicked soul

As the righteous soul do front line to the wicked soul, comfort and warm of wicked soul easy living so that wicked soul living easy living there for wicked soul do not do revenge and breaking energy, righteous soul survive living also possible.

But if righteous soul do not do front line

Then, how hard wicked soul living revenge and breaking, because wicked soul living do not feel easy living, so that wicked soul all anger and why not feel easy living so that wicked soul do use revenge and breaking.

Righteous soul front line is even for the wicked soul but truly for righteous soul.

This is creation of knowledge from righteous soul living in destination place, because righteous soul survive in the macro concept world only have to survive tools of "doing real love", so that righteous soul to survive righteous soul front line to the wicked soul is truly urgent, so that righteous soul do create front line to the wicked souls,

Wicked soul like to live at the righteous soul living front line so that righteous soul basic is warm but also comfortable with the harmony with other circumstance so that wicked soul living feel easy living, then righteous soul front line is done, righteous soul also in the front line help, as the wicked soul all sued up of wicked soul living, energy then, righteous soul feed righteous soul living energy to the wicked soul with righteous soul creation of knowledge.

This is excitement truth comes out

Before creation of knowledge heard that

Righteous soul do create front line is at first wicked soul feel in easy living, so that righteous soul do create harmony with other circumstance of front line, so that in the front line is so warm and comfortable, this is wicked soul feel easy living then, wicked soul just living so then as the righteous soul create this wicked soul feeling in easy living, then for a while righteous soul "the poor & righteous soul" of "righteous soul shares time with wicked soul and do help wicked soul learning creation of knowledge and doing real love of wicked soul" so then, righteous soul creating righteous soul energy, so direct to feed wicked soul righteous soul energy.

As the righteous soul also grow to the "righteous soul & nothing", but righteous soul front line of wicked soul living feeling in warm and comfortable so that here wicked soul also feed like infant of righteous soul, so that here is wicked soul changed into righteous soul baby, so then righteous soul do righteous soul behavior "it shares time with other, help other but also doing real love other" the energy also endless feed the baby of righteous soul in the righteous soul front line.

Here is righteous soul front line is

After meet before comes to the macro concept world, then righteous soul and wicked soul meet so that both comes to the macro concept world, so that soul room living, so this is front line created, so righteous soul survive in the soul rooms that is righteous soul living survive or not is decide.

Truly this is how to do, I did not know but today

Creation of knowledge make me learning it, this is righteous soul front line to the wicked soul, righteous soul create front line to the wicked soul, to make wicked soul feel warm and comfortable so that wicked soul feel easy living, then as the wicked soul feeling is easy living then, righteous soul also living in the soul room.

This is righteous soul create front line to the wicked soul

Then, wicked soul living easy living, so then righteous soul feed righteous living energy to the wicked soul so that, here is wicked soul to be changed into infant of righteous soul, so that righteous soul do "it shares time with other, help other, but also doing real love other"

So then, righteous soul energy all feed to the baby of wicked soul,

This is righteous soul living, feeding righteous soul energy to the wicked soul, but of righteous soul infant, this is truly righteous soul living mission in the soul room, for the purpose of righteous soul survive all of effort to do righteous soul behavior "it shares time with other, help other but also doing real love other".

Here is why righteous soul front line is creating is comes out.

Righteous soul do create front line to the wicked soul of "revenge and breaking", so that at first righteous soul crate do not use wicked soul "revenge and breaking" this is first because righteous soul first living in the soul room.

Infer that

Huge number of righteous soul fear of righteous soul "revenge and breaking" so that righteous soul did not do create front line to the wicked soul, so that automatically righteous soul disappeared in the soul room, so that automatically there is no righteous soul.

So that macro concept world living all wicked soul living actors so that macro concept world all to be living of "revenge and breaking" others, so that living there is no "it shares time with other, help other but also doing real love other".

In the end righteous soul livings are hard to survive in the macro concept world.

Infer that all of righteous soul disappeared in the macro concept world, so that in the macro concept world living all living is try to be easy living, so that the livings all of knowledge is from old knowledge.

Truly old knowledge useless solving now problems so that all of living in the problem

So that righteous soul front line wicked soul feel easy living, and feed righteous soul living energy with creation of knowledge getting to the wicked soul, now righteous soul infant so that righteous soul survive, then survive righteous soul as the "righteous soul & nothing " so that righteous soul living in the macro concept world, then, in the macro concept world righteous soul do righteous soul living behavior "it shares time with other, help other and doing real love other"

So that righteous soul survive then, macro concept world all to be changed into righteous soul livings circumstance, this is all from righteous soul me.

So that righteous soul must survive from wicked soul, for this survive from wicked soul, righteous soul front line is really required.

What is righteous soul front line?

Righteous soul front line

This is righteous soul living with wicked soul

Here is righteous soul created at the righteous soul living in destination place, in the righteous soul living in destination place, the living has been living silent and clean clear living of creation of knowledge living in excitement.

But righteous soul start voyage to the way of micro concept world way to the macro concept world, then truly infer righteous soul do not know how to go to the macro concept world, but also on the way to the macro concept world micro concept world wicked soul, this is do not know to the righteous soul, but on the way to the macro concept world, righteous soul live with wicked soul, this at first righteous soul front line with wicked soul.

Wicked soul living has been living in the wicked soul living in destination place,

Wicked soul living was loudly and dirty out of order old knowledge why I'm living on this wicked soul living In destination place, so that wicked soul try to do made me living in this living so that so anger but also living with wicked souls, in the wicked soul living all "revenge and breaking" so that "wicked soul" purpose to travel to macro concept world is anger express of revenge and breaking.

Righteous soul living voyage to the macro concept world is

Righteous soul living in destination place was so excitement place, beyond macro concept world living place, all righteous souls are doing "it shares time with righteous souls help righteous soul but also doing real love righteous" in the righteous soul living in destination place living is really excitement place, so that righteous soul voyage to macro concept world, to bring lover to this righteous soul living in destination place

Righteous soul mission also find lover of wicked soul, then doing real love of lover of wicked soul, righteous soul do real love of a new creation of righteous soul, and bring the lover of righteous soul to the righteous soul living in destination place.

What is righteous soul front line?

Front line is meeting

Wicked soul revenge and breaking and righteous soul doing real love

In this place righteous soul survive and wicked soul create to righteous soul

This is why reluctant to voyage to macro concept world?

Righteous soul voyage to macro concept world is originality righteous soul living is not traveling but voyage to do,

In the point of wicked soul even anger in the wicked soul living, but wicked soul must be here hard opportunity as new and again macro concept world voyage complete, then wicked soul truly depend on old knowledge, so that wicked soul do not know, how to macro concept world voyage complete

But wicked soul do not know even this, wicked soul now living is anger of revenge and breaking, so that this living in the macro concept world as did so then the living opportunity new living, creating to righteous soul living all gone, so again to the wicked soul living in destination place.

Wicked soul living create a new righteous soul as being righteous soul living with creation of knowledge, truly wicked soul also seek how to do,

So then wicked soul in this macro concept world meet before comes to macro concept world righteous soul is planned way, this is already cosmos law know it, but truly righteous soul is just meet lover in the macro concept world, but cosmos law know it

Wicked soul even anger revenge and breaking in the macro concept world, but righteous soul doing real love lover of wicked soul, so then cosmos law is wicked soul must be saved by righteous soul

So then cosmos law know it

Righteous soul is role of save wicked soul from wicked soul livings

This is righteous soul living role in the voyage macro concept world

Oh!

Surprised to me now

Righteous soul voyage function is to save wicked soul to righteous soul

So that righteous soul create front line for wicked souls

In the macro concept world wicked soul duty function of regulation,

Righteous soul is macro concept world create wicked soul righteous soul, yes this is in the dong real love of wicked soul lover to righteous soul lover saying.

Righteous soul living in the macro concept world is originality is righteous soul living itself is save wicked soul living to righteous soul living creature.

Who know this principle?

So then how hard righteous soul wicked soul a new create righteous soul, righteous soul is also in the created at a righteous soul creator same as now in the macro concept world righteous soul living is in the end, wicked soul to be created righteous soul living.

Righteous soul living creating wicked soul to righteous soul, but also wicked soul to be righteous soul by righteous soul doing real love, Righteous soul creator but wicked soul righteous soul's object to be a new creating righteous soul. Macro concept world voyage purpose is now saying.

Righteous soul role of helper wicked soul to be righteous soul

Wicked soul role to be righteous soul with living righteous soul, wicked soul is also urgent to be changed into righteous soul, this righteous soul doing real love.

So that righteous soul do real love wicked soul

But also wicked soul to be created to righteous soul, this is real living, but also cosmos law know it.

But if righteous soul do not survive then who save wicked soul, so then macro concept world there is no righteous soul, then automatically the place living is all wicked soul living, so then, in the righteous soul living is not, naturally the place is wicked soul living in destination place.

Why this book try to say "What is righteous soul front line?

Why now book writer try to help righteous soul living surviving here it is

Righteous soul living is the space and time is righteous soul living in destination place, but also righteous soul do create wicked soul to righteous soul, because wicked soul living failed macro concept world voyage did not complete, so then, it must be wicked soul can't living complete macro concept world, so that righteous soul help to live how to live is macro concept world voyage complete is righteous soul do helping being creature of wicked soul to be living in righteous soul living, then the wicked soul to be complete of macro concept world voyage.

Here is righteous soul is create front line to save wicked soul to righteous soul, but also righteous soul create lover of wicked soul to righteous soul so then, righteous soul also get a righteous soul of lover.

So that righteous soul mission clear in the macro concept voyage, for this righteous soul front line to the wicked soul is, really righteous soul living principle, this is righteous soul living of real living.

Righteous soul living front line of circumstance to the wicked soul

Righteous soul is circumstance to the wicked soul living.

Righteous soul feels living in silent and clean clear living is excitement living.

But wicked soul living is loudly and dirty of residue of past happened so that righteous soul it must be do not like wicked soul living in the righteous soul circumstance.

But wicked soul move and anger and even a sharp all of dangerous behavior brining and used in the circumstance of righteous soul.

So that righteous soul do real love to the wicked soul, this is righteous soul doing real love, so that righteous soul all undertake of wicked soul all of behavior, wicked souls feeling is all changeable, just like weather all the time is not same, but strange wicked soul do not know creation of knowledge but only know is old knowledge, so that to the righteous soul me, all supplied past trade memory this is helping to the mind level living actors, so that here is wicked soul and mind is friend, but this is all loudly and dirty living possible in the circumstance of righteous soul.

Righteous soul circumstance is originality is clean clear and silent excitement but to the righteous soul feeling silent and clean clear excitement is so hard because wicked soul livings; wicked soul do not runs for the create of knowledge but old knowledge which all knowledge is mixed with mind and wicked soul livings contaminate so that the old knowledge is just like before happen residue and old learned knowledge so that wicked soul living based on old knowledge, so that anger to the residue of before a wicked souls do not like me or deceit me or do not do righteous soul livings all of wicked soul feel anger so that wicked soul push me to do repay, this is really important righteous soul livings all do not follow of wicked soul anger, and past residue but do not living in righteous soul follow to the wicked soul past knowledge of residue, this is result of behavior wicked soul "revenge and breaking" so that macro concept world me being actor of wicked soul living.

Righteous soul circumstance of wicked soul living

Righteous soul circumstance is even though wicked souls are living, thoroughly if righteous soul circumstance is silent and clean clear then, righteous soul keep supplied to macro concept world me, but truly all of living are strong wicked soul, but also all of macro concept world living behavior is not burnt all of behavior, if all perfect burnt but also cleans water, then in the circumstance of righteous soul feel silent and clean clear of excitement.

But macro concept world living me behavior is do not do righteous soul living so that mind living and wicked soul living therefore of mind and wicked soul living residue accumulate as did righteous soul circumstance is all contaminate of macro concept world mind and wicked soul living residue is accumulate as did, righteous soul try to do silent and clean clear but in this place is loudly and dirty residue is filled so that righteous soul want to live of silent and clean clear is hard.

Righteous soul circumstance is being polluted

Righteous soul circumstance all dirty and loudly of wicked soul so that, the macro concept living actor is automatically wicked soul living behavior how wicked soul living me excitement because relative with old knowledge which is related with paste accident residue and dirty trash in the circumstance of righteous soul.

So that righteous soul circumstance all defunct because all of dirty and loudly so that all forgotten righteous soul circumstance, so that all of circumstance is full of residue of trash of paste accident, truly righteous soul like silent and clean clear but wicked soul all did bring a past do not all burnt, just half burnt residue, in the righteous soul living in destination place all of past is closed so that past is past, so that to be live in the righteous soul living, silent and clean clear so that past perfect burnt, keep silent and clean clear of creation of knowledge, here is creation of knowledge is perfect is not connect to past, but wicked soul living is "easy living" so that already existence knowledge so that wicked soul super of old knowledge, but wicked soul living best on the past old knowledge, wicked soul living is based on old knowledge living.

But righteous soul living based on creation of knowledge this is all new and frame of creation of knowledge is not strong, but also wicked soul old knowledge is power but righteous soul of creation of knowledge is not strong.

But wicked soul do not know righteous soul creation of knowledge to be old knowledge, so that this righteous soul creation of knowledge is variance macro concept world but also a new living making but wicked soul keep stuck a creation of knowledge comes, so that wicked soul keep supplied to the righteous soul circumstance.

Wicked soul old knowledge

Righteous soul creation of knowledge

Why creation of knowledge create creation of knowledge macro concept world livings this is this, if living of wicked soul is all of dirty and loudly old knowledge all accumulate in the righteous soul circumstance, so that macro concept world wicked soul is full of old knowledge of residue of past living accident so that, righteous soul do not live silent and clean clear living, so that righteous soul do not supplied to the macro concept world wicked soul righteous soul creation of knowledge.

But to the righteous soul of there is no residue of past relative old knowledge, but all of past is closed righteous soul feel silent and clean clear then, righteous soul supplied to the macro concept righteous soul me, a creation of knowledge who runs to the righteous soul living in destination place.

Righteous soul circumstance is clean clear but also silent here is no wicked soul and mind me, so called there is no mind, there is no me, mind 1/ and the poor & righteous soul, but also righteous soul & nothing.

Righteous soul is nothing, so that nothing of righteous soul runs to the righteous soul living in destination place, righteous soul creation of knowledge is from righteous soul living in destination place, this is all problems solving of running to the righteous soul living in destination place, so then, wicked soul used creation of knowledge after pass the place, so that wicked soul do not catch righteous soul, righteous soul meet in the front line also, righteous soul and wicked soul problems also all solved by the righteous soul creation of knowledge.

Righteous soul circumstance to the wicked soul behavior

Righteous soul to be all of wicked soul mind level residue of past accident then, the actor must be wicked soul living in the macro concept world.

So that wicked soul and mind level living is all fills with residue of paste relative mind will how to get money to rent money so this is all automatically the old knowledge wicked soul supplied as the analysis all of it, so that wicked soul and mind living is very easy living.

But to the righteous soul living "it shares time with other, help other, but also doing real love other" it never do by the wicked soul old knowledge, because in this wicked soul analysis there is no help other, this is in the righteous soul living behavior so that

As the all of residue of old knowledge and residue of past accident are all past relatives it is strange all good burnt do not anger is not but all half burnt and reside is "revenge and breaking" energy of wicked soul is strong living.

This is true wicked soul do not know all good and burnt there is no any problems past all forget but half burnt past knowledge all push macro concept me, then wicked soul push me to do something, then here is really make me the wicked souls slaver of actor.

So then all fix to the past behavior

This is do nor living of righteous soul living, righteous soul living to be that all of residue of past must be all righteous soul feel that push to me, then righteous soul me all "forgive the think of wicked soul and sent to the cosmos law court all of this the name of Jesus Christ amen", righteous soul me keep clean righteous circumstance to be silent and clean clear.

Macro concept world righteous soul me

Help righteous soul, so that macro concept world righteous soul do not live wicked soul living but also do not living of mind level living, but also all live of righteous soul living behavior "it shares time with other, help other but also doing real love other"

Then, all of new and clean clear of righteous soul living energy input to righteous soul circumstance then, in the dirty and loudly of wicked soul livings to be cleaned by the righteous soul living energy

Macro concept world front line righteous soul living me to wicked soul livings

Macro concept world living is voyage living to be going to micro concept world.

Micro concept world living feeling is now seen world of macro concept world is voyage living, but do not know micro concept world then, the livings are all destination living, so that micro concept world living and macro concept world destination living is not same.

Micro concept world livings are all try to safe and complete voyage in the macro concept world then safe returning to micro concept world righteous soul living in destination place.

Bur macro concept world is destination living s are living, then feel of macro concept world is destination livings are all living try to "easy living"; getting good positon, and getting good and much more than other positon, to be all of "revenge and breaking energy using" so that same portion but wicked soul has power to oppress others, because they all feeling in this is destination living, but also this living end is all to be feeling of macro concept world end is "dead".

But feeling micro concept world righteous souls are not, they all now living is voyage, so that righteous soul living s are all running voyage, so that righteous soul living now, is voyage mission "find the wicked soul of lover then do real love wicked soul lover then create righteous soul, so that love to be righteous soul then, here voyage ne of macro concept world then safe returning to the righteous soul living in destination" this living is righteous soul

Righteous souls are creating front line creating a creation of circumstance lover of wicked soul coms to me, then living excitement in righteous soul front line, this is for the purpose of righteous soul mission on voyage in the macro concept world.

Righteous soul macro concept world voyage mission is doing create wicked soul to righteous soul, so called macro concept world expression, do save from wicked soul to righteous soul, here is then wicked soul anger, but micro concept do create wicked soul to righteous soul, to be that righteous soul front line for the wicked soul.

Here is in the righteous soul front line, a wicked soul also feel that macro concept world is to the wicked soul is very precious opportunity, wicked soul feel really urgent, wicked soul truly do not know macro concept world is only voyage but as the righteous soul front line, doing real love with helping knowing wicked soul creation of knowledge, which is to the wicked soul is here is chance to live in the micro concept world righteous soul living in destination place, so that righteous soul help knowing how to complete voyage, then this is wicked soul to be righteous soul creation.

This is here it is righteous soul front line to wicked soul

Here is righteous soul front line to wicked soul is even righteous soul macro concept world voyage mission but to the wicked soul is precious chance to be living righteous soul living, so that righteous soul helper to the wicked soul to be living in righteous soul, so wicked soul know that wicked soul know that in the micro concept world living was so hard, not hard but the living is not living, the living is a kind of wicked souls of den; the place is adverse to the righteous soul living in destination place, dirty loudly and do not do living with other, do not help other, but also do not do real love other. Truly living is doing not express can't living, if possible all exodus from wicked soul.

At last now macro concept world is must be again chance to not to going to the wicked soul but to go righteous soul, so that here macro concept world living must be complete this is super important for the wicked soul opportunity not to be again living at the wicked soul living in destination place, so that macro concept world is changed so precious s opportunity.

Righteous soul to wicked soul some of different, but all has the urgent macro concept world is wicked soul and righteous soul all opportunity,

So then sure of know micro concept world then both wicked soul and righteous souls living is urgent to be macro concept world have to do, but do not know micro concept world, living in the macro concept world destination living, so that they do not know macro concept world living is voyage living.

Righteous soul front line is

Righteous soul is doing "it shares time with wicked soul, and help wicked soul, and doing real love wicked soul", so then righteous soul living doing righteous soul living behavior, here is macro concept world righteous soul living with wicked soul and mind level livings, mind level livings are do not know micro concept world living, so that they are all living here is destination living.

But righteous soul living feeling that this living is only voyage living, so that in the time is comes then automatically shift from macro concept world to micro concept world, so then righteous soul livings doing excitement safe returning to the righteous soul living, that is home coming, all of already known righteous souls all welcome of macro concept world safe complete voyage but also, safe returning righteous soul bring an eternity living lover also bring to the righteous soul living in destination place.

So here is righteous soul hear broadcasting from righteous soul, then here saying, macro concept world dong real love and creature, this is righteous soul do righteous soul create lover, then this is originality this is preparing living in eternity in the righteous soul, so that in the voyage meeting a wicked soul of lover, then all of macro concept world righteous soul create lover of righteous soul, truly in the micro concept world can't meet lover, because here all living eternity is get lover hetero of lover, so that wicked soul is righteous souls of wicked soul to create righteous soul, so then created lover of righteous soul and righteous soul me is strong lover feeling.

So that righteous soul living is urgent because after voyage macro concept world, then soon living in the micro concept world eternity living, then meet a wicked soul and creating righteous soul is how hard to the righteous soul, but righteous soul do, here is again wicked soul also so urgent to be living complete macro concept world.

To the wicked soul also know that macro concept world voyage complete, so wicked soul also do not again comes to this hard living, so then wicked soul also must be urgent, but if do not meet and invite in the righteous soul front line, then the wicked soul must be living after again to the wicked soul living in destination place.

So that wicked soul so living at a hard and difficult of torture of wicked soul again living, truly wicked soul is try to living "easy living" is so hard in the wicked soul living so that simply, wicked soul living in the macro concept world "easy living", if wicked soul do living easy living then, macro living after again fall to the wicked soul, so that, here is macro concept world living is how important it is.

Macro concept world living is righteous soul front line is must be infer that husband wife living of marriage, so then this is how important it is here comes, each living free in the macro concept world, then, marriage living is both to be living in the micro concept world, so that macro concept world voyage is must be for the purpose of micro concept world righteous soul living in destination place living, so then both righteous soul, and wicked soul all to be living in excitement, but this is not, because wicked soul "revenge and breaking" and righteous soul "doing real love" this is originality is impossible, but both living is must be know that here living is not destination place.

Righteous soul front line to the wicked soul lover, then

Righteous soul dong real love with creation of knowledge lover of wicked soul, then even revenge and breaking wicked soul also know that, because wicked soul also change here macro concept world from wicked soul to righteous soul, then here is wicked soul try to be living after macro concept world voyage, so that wicked soul of lover also adsorb righteous soul doing real love and creation of knowledge, so that wicked soul also try to be living of righteous soul "wicked soul do shares time with righteous soul, and helping and doing real love to the righteous soul" so that righteous soul also living with wicked soul, but also wicked soul living with righteous soul.

Then here is righteous soul living survive from wicked soul fear of revenge breaking energy, but also wicked soul doing loved from righteous soul dong real loving, so that wicked soul feel so excitement, so that wicked soul do not use wicked soul energy, but also wicked soul do not get more energy of wicked soul, this is spontaneity do not do wicked soul energy depend on but rely on the righteous soul dong real love, but also all depend on righteous soul behavior "righteous soul do share time with lover of wicked soul and help lover of wicked soul and dong real love lover of wicked soul", so then wicked soul also to be being righteous soul living is best but also in the end this macro concept world living finish then, automatically shift to the righteous soul living in destination place living.

This is wicked soul living macro concept world living is really opportunity time for the wicked souls to be changed into righteous soul living, in the macro concept world all of livings same chance to living change to righteous soul, so here is very important is, righteous souls create front line for the lover of wicked soul, to create lover of righteous soul so that righteous soul doing real love of front line to the wicked soul is righteous soul living so hard, so that righteous soul as possible as can do not do again macro concept world voyage, so safe returned righteous souls all welcome because they know that how hard living in the macro concept world living.

Here is macro concept world is bot righteous soul and wicked soul all to be living is so hard, because righteous soul living dong real love is must be used for the wicked soul create righteous soul, but also wicked soul so urgent chance so that wicked soul also this macro concept world living is really precious opportunity to chance to create living of righteous soul living, so that macro concept world living complete not any more voyage to the macro concept world so that macro concept world living do righteous soul living is urgent.

Righteous soul is space of circumstance

This book front line and space of circumstance is beginning as micro concept world mixed with watching in me, then who is righteous soul but here is think of wicked soul feel change but who is righteous soul, who is not changed.

Then here is righteous soul is eternity do not change, this is righteous soul living, then here is do not changed truth, means that righteous soul is same as the 5000 years ago in a person in world righteous soul and now righteous soul me, also same, do not changed but just with living wicked soul who are all just second changed, so that wicked soul feel good worse all of changed feeling, but righteous soul do not changed feeling, this is same in the righteous soul living in destination place or here is macro concept world living me in righteous soul is same.

So then, here is do not changed righteous soul is being "righteous soul is space of circumstances to changeable wicked soul, so that righteous soul is front line to live wicked soul in the righteous soul space of circumstance.

After all this book "righteous soul living "front line" "is that defined of righteous soul is being wicked soul living space of circumstance.

Until 16 books writing I said righteous and wicked soul, but truly wicked soul is defined as the "think of wicked soul", which is moving and a second changing feeling is variance so that wicked soul is moving in me.

But which is righteous soul, the just this book "righteous soul living "front lie"" is defined that righteous soul is space of circumstance to the wicked soul, so that righteous soul is just like a bowl, bur water is wicked soul compared.

"Righteous soul living front line" = "Righteous soul is space of circumstance"

Here is righteous soul to be warm and excitement for wicked souls, then wicked soul is also to be feel warm and excitement, then righteous soul do righteous soul living behavior "it shares time with wicked soul, help wicked soul, but also doing real love wicked soul in the front line; righteous soul space circumstance"

This is righteous soul living, righteous soul is living as the poor & righteous soul, then, the living is try to be distance from wicked soul, but if righteous soul to be living as "the righteous soul & nothing" then, here is righteous soul actively and push fully front line with wicked soul for the purpose of righteous soul mission carry; righteous soul meet lover of wicked soul and doing real love wicked soul to create righteous soul, this space of circumstance is now saying this book " righteous soul living "front line".

Righteous soul living "front line"

I'm so tired with book writing.

This book "righteous soul living "front line" is a kind of challenge book, I try to find and saying, righteous soul is eternity living of creation of knowledge source, but also righteous soul is space and circumstance.

Why I'm tried to say this who read my book?

Until now book wrote 16 books but truly these books are not give me excitement, book is my source of doing not in excitement, so that on today hurry comes my work place, yesterday built new book based I did before erased, then rather seek who am I how to live this is real in now.

This book "righteous soul living "front line"

Now closing

Truly book writing is hard

Because book writing and book publish and readers reading

So that still my book is not it now book, because my all books are not read

Because my 16 books are not signal to me "my creator I'm living well"

Here is 17 book now will birth

When I can to be feeling in excitement?

When my living is normal living?

At now my time is am 5:53

My routine is comes early and do book writing is my real excitement but truly now I'm tired.

It must be book writing is out of excitement, why I'm living like that

Truly this is my way, book writing.

"Righteous soul" this is my only saying, my book protagonist so then what I doing is this, truly I'm not a book writer but only what I can do is "righteous soul"

These days righteous soul "me" run to other place

So that book writing is also, truly in me, there is no righteous soul, so that I'm losing righteous soul.

On today this book "righteous soul living "front line" will finish.

Righteous soul is front line with wicked soul, so that always righteous soul and wicked soul is front line, micro concept world righteous soul living in destination place and wicked soul living in destination is not same, but here is body of macro concept world micro concept of righteous soul wicked soul is front line living.

Righteous soul and wicked soul is coincident living.

Righteous soul must be not bored cause of front line of wicked soul variable.

Wicked soul is fast changed, good to bad, bad to good, but righteous soul is do not changed eternity living of truth, so that here is so hard which is righteous soul?

This book try saying righteous soul is space, righteous soul is circumstance, Righteous soul also do see moving wicked souls who are all to be changed.

So then righteous soul is space, originality righteous soul is space so that this space is not fill is best to the righteous soul, but if righteous soul space all of residue of unburnt past relatives so that righteous soul space all to be dirty and loudly and waste and garbage so that righteous soul space is so polluted.

Then righteous soul is space so then, righteous soul living is living in the waste dumping ground, if then righteous soul space is not righteous soul silent and clean clear of creation of knowledge is not created, this is wicked soul living in destination place, so then righteous soul living front line is impossible.

There is no silent clean clear in me, so then how to know righteous soul front line, even my readers all to be bored what it is ?

But truly if righteous soul there is no wicked soul, but here is all righteous soul, so that righteous soul silent and clean clear then, here righteous soul do front line to the wicked soul, because here is righteous soul is silent and clean clear so then here is "righteous soul & nothing", so that righteous soul living is feeling is all excitement.

Righteous soul soon to be safe returning to the righteous soul living in destination place, so that righteous soul is reach at the perfect righteous soul it really clean clear and silent is righteous soul & nothing

So that righteous soul do front line wicked soul, and in the front line, righteous soul righteous soul living behavior of "it shares time with other, help other, but also doing real love other", so that as dimple doing to the wicked soul do righteous soul living behavior then, wicked soul created from wicked soul to righteous souls.

So then righteous soul can did mission clear

Righteous soul living mission is "righteous soul meet lover of wicked soul, then as the righteous soul doing real love of righteous soul living behavior then, lover of wicked soul to be righteous soul of lover and bring lover of righteous soul to the righteous soul living in destination place" righteous soul & nothing mission clear.

Righteous soul do mission clear then, it required to be righteous soul & nothing, there is no any wicked soul but only righteous soul, because in the righteous soul living front line, wicked soul to be righteous soul, so then, righteous souls do living silent and clean clear so that both righteous soul and lover of righteous soul living is silent and clean clear.

This living is already being righteous soul macro concept world voyage complete.

Righteous soul complete macro concept world voyage complete.

Righteous soul stay at the righteous soul living in destination place eternity living with lover of righteous soul, both righteous souls living in excitement in the righteous soul living in destination place, this is Righteous soul living "front line" righteous soul silent and clean clear make it possible.

Printed in the United States
By Bookmasters